# Unfinished Business

## Journal of an Embattled European

For Malcolm + Colan.

For all our futures

Geraint Talfryn

Llanedeyrn

Caerdydd

2018

Read 30/10/18

# Unfinished Business

## Journal of an Embattled European

Geraint Talfan Davies

Foreword by
David Marquand

Parthian, Cardigan SA43 1ED
www.parthianbooks.com
First published in 2018
© Geraint Talfan Davies
ISBN 978-1-912681-07-5
Cover design: www.theundercard.co.uk
Typeset by Elaine Sharples
Printed and bound by Pulsio
Published with the financial support of the Welsh Books Council
A cataloguing record for this book is available from the British Library.

*This book is for our eight European grandchildren*
*Harri, Bea, Ethan, Oscar, Layla, Sam, Nye, Eliot*

# CONTENTS

# FOREWORD

Geraint Talfan Davies has played a pivotal role in the cultural, intellectual and political life of Wales for the best part of forty years. He was the co-founder of the Institute of Welsh Affairs – part think-tank, part research centre and, at its best, a forum for wide-ranging, challenging debate involving politicians, writers, academics and representatives of civil society bodies of all kinds. He is a prolific journalist, with a gift for deadly put-downs and cutting wit. (I particularly enjoyed his description of Nigel Farage as a 'saloon bar Saladin' and of Boris Johnson as the 'Bullingdon bugle'.) He has been a ubiquitous presence in the musical life of Wales, as Chair of the Welsh National Opera and Governor of the Welsh College of Music and Drama. He has chaired the Arts Council of Wales and the Cardiff Bay Arts Trust; he has also served as a board member of the Wales Millennium Centre. For him high culture of this sort is intrinsic to the civic culture on which pluralist democracy depends. Above all, he has been a forensically deadly and emotionally uplifting champion of European unity, with Britain in general and Wales in particular playing the fullest possible roles in the construction of a just and democratic Europe.

Too often, debate about Britain's relationship with the rest of the European continent has been fatally lop-sided. Again and again, Yeats's terrible lines in *The Second Coming* – 'The best lack all conviction, while the worst/ Are full of passionate intensity' – have seemed hideously apposite. The motley crew of Brexiteers, from Gisela Stuart to Boris Johnson, from David Owen to David Davis, from Andrea Leadsom to Michael Gove, and from Chris Grayling to the preposterous Jacob Rees-Mogg have been brimming over with passionate intensity. All too often the Remainers have looked and sounded as if they lack conviction. David Cameron's campaign during the referendum debate was not just lacklustre; it was positively comatose. De-coded, his premise was that membership of the European Union was a pretty dreadful fate, but a mite less dreadful than non-membership. Of Jeremy Corbyn and John McDonnell, it is kinder not to speak. Their answer to the Johnson-Gove myth of glorious isolation á la Lord Salisbury is a myth of socialism in one country á la Joseph Stalin. Against that background the most surprising feature of the EU referendum result is that so many commentators were surprised by it.

Talfan Davies's *Journal of an Embattled European* is a heart-warming antidote – a breath of fresh air in a foetid atmosphere of self-deception, misrepresentation and downright mendacity. He is a European of the head. Again and again he shows how much British firms, British workers and British investors gain from EU membership – and how much self-exile from the world's second largest economy will cost, not least to Wales. In his final chapter he quotes approvingly a CBI study showing that all possible alternatives to EU membership will make life more difficult for exporters, for citizens of the most disadvantaged regions of the United Kingdom and, above all, for the peoples both of Northern Ireland and of the Irish Republic.

But he is, above all, a European of the heart. His diary begins with an under-stated, but (as a result) heart-wrenchingly moving account of a visit to Auschwitz-Birkenau. He doesn't point the obvious moral, but he doesn't need to: the monstrous genocide that the Nazi regime perpetrated against the Jewish people was the darkest of the demons that Jean Monnet, the chief architect of the European project, hoped and believed European unity would exorcise. One of the most powerful entries in his *Journal* is entitled 'Europe Means Us'. The Brexiteers' notion that 'our kingdom's watery boundary creates an ineradicable distinction between us and our continental brothers and sisters', he points out, is simply untrue.

For centuries we were part of the Roman Empire. For a millennium we were fully part of Catholic Europe. Our Protestantism was derived from elsewhere in northern Europe. An instinct for standing aloof has not prevented us from being drawn into wars with Spain, France, Italy and Germany. In the twentieth century we were not able to stand aside from Europe's two civil wars, the bloodiest in history. For the last half century, the European Union has preserved an unprecedented internal peace by focusing on our common interests and weaving common solutions... In the process we extended democracy to millions.

So what should we do? Talfan Davies's diary is not a manifesto. It is a call to arms. 'Resistance', he writes, 'is not undemocratic'. Referendums are not – cannot be – sacrosanct. Continuous challenge is of democracy's essence. The greatest political leaders and thinkers in the western canon – from Pericles and Abraham Lincoln to Alexis de Tocqueville and Amartya Sen – would agree. It is up to Talfan Davies's readers to heed his call.

David Marquand
April 2018

# INTRODUCTION

Involvement in journalism and broadcasting means that you are in daily touch with the nation's conversation, yet I cannot recall any period of my life when the conversation was so dominated by one subject, nor one that has caused such a deep rift in our society. Since the late 1960s I have always been passionately engaged in the devolution debate, but compared with the matter of membership of the European Union that was a minority sport. The 2016 referendum divided families – even husbands from wives – and, two years later, from time to time friends still occasionally have to agree not to discuss the subject over a drink or a meal. Brexit has been all-consuming. For every seventeen people who voted to leave the European Union, sixteen voted to remain. That is how narrow the vote was, but it is a rift that remains to this day.

One thing that the Remain side discovered to its cost during the 2016 referendum was that transactional arguments do not always prevail. Whatever else it was, the response of Leave voters was not based on accountancy. For Remain voters the referendum result was an existential threat. For that reason I make no excuse for setting out my own responses to the issue with a necessary ration of emotion.

Europe has been threaded through my life, sometimes consciously, sometimes subconsciously, since my birth. My father had to seek out a new career during the Second World War, having seen his Swansea pharmacy and his home destroyed in the blitz. My earliest memories of political events, as a twelve-year-old, were around Britain's Suez debacle and, in the same year, the Soviet invasion of Hungary. As a teenage schoolboy my first overseas visit was to Rome in 1960 to see the Olympic Games, having had first to measure out a meagre ration of foreign currency. In the sixties, as a student at Oxford, and long before de Gaulle's veto on our membership, I heard Edward Heath lecture persuasively on Europe. The same year student friends and I drove across Europe through what was then Yugoslavia to Greece. The plight of the Balkans and of Greece mean so much more as a result.

In 1968, long before the days of twenty-four-hour television news, and by now a trainee journalist, I remember the depressing telexes that told of another Soviet invasion, this time of Czechoslovakia. In the run up to the 1975 referendum my newspaper, the *Western Mail*, sent me on briefing trips to Brussels, briefings that I had the privilege to share with the late Hugo Young, whose work, *This Blessed Plot*, charted the insular timorousness of our relationship with Europe. I also eked out the meagre salary of a provincial journalist by writing pro-Europe pamphlets at the behest of the late Gwyn Morgan who, after failing to be made General Secretary of the Labour Party, on the casting vote of Tony Benn, went to Brussels to assist the British Commissioner, George Thomson, to establish powerful regional policies. It was Gwyn and his Welsh colleague at the Commission,

Aneurin Rhys Hughes, who insisted on setting up EEC offices in Wales and Scotland. A second privilege was to be able to learn from another distinguished journalist, Neal Ascherson, during a visit to Germany to study regional government, ahead of the 1979 referendums on devolution in Scotland and Wales. His insights into Poland and other East European countries were always telling and poignant. In Germany again, this time for a British Army briefing – strangely, during the Falklands War – a helicopter visit to the Iron Curtain was a visceral experience. In retrospect it all seemed a prelude to the fall of the Berlin Wall, and a very different Europe. But more telling than all these experiences has been the fact that my eldest son married a Danish woman who had worked in Wales for a decade and a half and set up a business here. Their two children have, since the referendum, also been registered as Danish citizens. Our family is and always will be, inextricably, a European family.

For all these reasons involvement in our current debate has been unavoidable, frustrating though much of it has been. During the referendum campaign Lord Dafydd Wigley and I represented Wales on the Board of Britain Stronger In. He represented Plaid Cymru and I was there as Chair of the Wales Advisory Group. There was no shortage of effort by the campaign staff, but one was left with the impression of a highly centralised campaign in which all the instructions were coming from 10 Downing Street. This was echoed in the fact that campaign staff in Wales had all been recruited before any Wales Advisory Group was put in place. It was certainly under-resourced to run a pan-Wales campaign, especially in circumstances where Welsh political parties were all but exhausted after a year of campaigning for Assembly elections. Our group had to buy in additional resource hurriedly. There were certainly tensions between London and Cardiff at staff level that were never entirely resolved.

That experience has been one of the reasons why, when Wales for Europe was established after the referendum, it chose to take a more autonomous route, although still remaining part of the successor Open Britain campaign. The relationship between Cardiff and London is now open and constructive. We have been able to benefit from the central resource while shaping our campaign within Wales in our own way. We have been able to retain access to the large database of supporters across Wales that was gleaned during the referendum.

Many of these pieces were written as newspaper columns, but some were a response to other imperatives. One had to write *A Tourist in Auschwitz* after a visit that took place at the end of Poland's first year as a member of the European Union. *A disfiguring event* charts my own despair at the referendum result. *Single Market of the Mind* summarises a research project undertaken for the Institute of Welsh Affairs following an emotional meeting of cultural organisations in Swansea early in 2017, arranged by the Creative Industries Federation, the British Council and the Arts Council of Wales. *Ireland – perils of amnesia* expresses embarrassment and sorrow at what we may be about to inflict on our closest Western neighbour. *Self praise is no recommendation* and *Unfinished Business* both deal with aspects of our imperial hangover. The latter also tackles the pivotal role of the Labour Party.

Many of the columns were published in the *Western Mail* and in *Agenda*, the journal of the Institute of Welsh Affairs. I am therefore grateful to successive Directors of the IWA – John Osmond, Lee Waters and Auriol Miller. I must also thank Catrin Pascoe, editor of the *Western Mail*, not only for space in her paper but also for a more balanced coverage of the Europe debate than in the bulk of the London press. Hope springs eternal, so I have not altered predictions where events have proved me wrong.

None of this would have been possible without the willing commitment of so many volunteers. It would be fair to say that the initiative in setting up Wales for Europe came first from a small group of people in Swansea, alarmed that Swansea was one of the few university cities that voted Leave. By now there are local groups in Cardiff, Swansea, Newport, the south Wales valleys and north Wales, with more being formed as I write. We have a part-time Director, Helen Birtwhistle, who has brought great energy and skill to the task. Peter Gilbey has also been hugely creative as well as indefatigable in managing our events, website and social media presence. I wish to thank all our supporters who are giving their time unstintingly. I must also thank those from whom I have received both friendship and invaluable advice: Hywel Ceri Jones, Professor Kevin Morgan and David Melding AM. I am also hugely grateful to David Marquand not only for his generous foreword to this book but also for his ever energetic and inspiring contributions to the debate. Above all, our campaign would have not have been possible without the generous and enthusiastic support of David and Heather Stevens, whose commitment to my own community seems to know no bounds.

Lastly, I have to thank my wife, Elizabeth, who has borne my enthusiasms over the years with a patience and support no man has a right to expect – and on Europe, is as bloody angry as I am.

Geraint Talfan Davies
29 March 2018

# PRELUDE

## 30 April 2005

## A tourist at Auschwitz[1]

The weather seemed inappropriate: a warm and cloudless spring day breathed life into the ploughed fields and fallow strips, the sun slicing through stands of naked birch and beech. In the hedgeless fields a farmer following a horse-drawn plough told you this was not a rich country. Soon the fields retreated behind fresh kerbs and fences as we reached a small town of familiar and dreary modernity, ringed by the usual clutter of car showrooms and builders merchants. It was at the roundabout that we first saw the name – the strange, native, but unresonating name of Oswiecim, better know by the alien imposition, Auschwitz.

Our cheery conversation as travelling friends was snuffed out by unspoken apprehensions. On a road-side railway that would have attracted little attention in any other place, a passing line of freight wagons instantly carried other meanings for us all. The images are a

---

[1] First published in *Planet*, No. 174, 2005.

11

discomfiting part of our heritage: Hitler's famously prompt trains bringing millions from every corner of mainland Europe to an industrialised death. They arrived to be enslaved and 'selected'. We arrived at a neat, tarmac car park – cars to the right, coaches to the left. Auschwitz 1, first of the three camps. The first visible sign pointed to the 'Bar'.

Why were we here? One of our friends was not sure that we should have come. She knew more about Eastern Europe than any of us. The daughter of a British military attaché, she had lived in Prague during Dubcek's shortlived 'Spring' of 1968. Wasn't this just voyeurism, indulging in the pornography of violence? Wasn't it enough for us to know that Auschwitz existed, enough for us to have seen the documentaries and photographs and memorised the images on our own march down an endless avenue of wartime anniversaries? Wouldn't the greatest respect to the dead millions be to stay away? Isn't there something tasteless about including Auschwitz in a 'weekend city break'?

The answers seemed easy. Here is a place emblematic of the very worst that was done by man in the bloodiest century in history. We should not avert our eyes. The world has not only to remember but also to understand as fully as possible the enormity of this moral catastrophe. How could we come to the Polish city of Krakow and feast on the tourist's staple diet of castles and cathedrals, while quietly ignoring, on grounds of taste, the worst that had happened in anybody's lifetime, just down the road? How could we sip our beers sunnily in the 'largest medieval square in Europe', but flinch from the much bigger squares of barbed wire half an hour away? And if we did, how could we be sure it was out of respect for the dead rather than for our own leisured comfort? In the light of experience, the answers were more equivocal.

Even in off-peak April the ticket hall was full. Everyone sported a coloured badge to mark which language group they would join. We had arrived by ten o'clock in time for the short and harrowing English language film. The grainy images had none of the polish and sophistication of the BBC documentaries we had all seen; but who needs the film maker's art in the face of such reality? Such simple comparisons were a source of constant conflict throughout the visit: every failure to suppress the modern tourist's relativism creating discomfort, like a devout adolescent's guilt at failing to concentrate on God in church.

All our mental images of Auschwitz and the other camps are deeply imprinted. So the first shock is the familiarity: it is as if we have seen it all before. Those images are also all monochrome, so the second shock is colour. The grey blockhouses of newsreel footage are actually of dark red brick and roofed with red tiles – old barracks of a more conventional army. The rough spaces between the blockhouses where the striped slaves would have been marshalled or their corpses piled, are rectangles of bright green turf where, today, the sun glistened on the mower's neat suburban tracks. We wondered what measure of comfort the sun had brought to those with a fingernail's grip on life.

Primo Levi has the crushing answer: "We fought with all our strength to prevent the arrival of winter. We clung to all the warm hours, at every dusk we tried to keep the sun in the sky for a little longer, but it was all in vain. Yesterday evening the sun went down irrevocably behind a confusion of dirty clouds, chimney stacks and wires, and today it is winter. We know what it means because we were here last winter, and the others will soon learn. It means that in the course of these months from October to April, seven out of ten of us will die. Whoever does not die will suffer minute by minute, all day every day."

It is in one of the blockhouses that the residue of the dead seven out of ten are piled behind huge glass windows, against which hundreds of tourist-pilgrims jostle. Behind one a forty-foot long bank of lifeless hair, grey not only from age but also because shorn from traumatised, sick and starving people. One thicker, darker plait alone gave a hint of buried beauty. Behind another window a mass of wire spectacle frames – not a piece of conceptual art, but the tangled remains of the orderly destruction of real people; behind another, a vast bank of dusty shoes (that monochrome again), the occasional clog a tell-tale sign of the furthermost fields of a pitiless harvest. A pair of pale pink women's shoes stood out from the rest and I wondered whether it was these that had prompted Spielberg's heart-wrenching device in *Schindler's List* of creating one dab of pale colour on a little girl's coat in an otherwise black and white film.

Photographs of the un-named faces that owned these artefacts lined the walls of another blockhouse – the men and women separated, as they were in the camp itself. The faces of the women were haunting, seeming to show less fear than the men. Instead, I see a quiet defiance: firm chins, direct and penetrating eyes, the same mixture of disappointment, pity and reproach that they might have given to their own errant children. The men looked beaten. In the claustrophobic basement of the punishment block the crowd has funnelled into single file to peer into cells where the despair and sometimes the faith of the tortured and dying has been scratched into the walls. The desperation is beyond imagination. It is here that you sense visitors pushing themselves to the threshold of their own revulsion as they shuffle through. A clipped guide moves us on.

It is not easy to find space to digest one's own thoughts in Auschwitz 1. It is a tight campus, and even in April the crowds are large. As we move beneath the crazily familiar 'Arbeit Macht Frei' sign, a large man in one of the groups is licking a choc ice and seems oblivious to the circles of whispered disapproval around him. The guide remonstrates. He shrugs his shoulders and finds a bin. Numbers, as always, mean places of pilgrimage succumb to the tourism process, become part of the tourist's gaze: the car and coach parks, the groups, the in-your-face T-shirts, the digital cameras (including my own), the multi-lingual commentaries, the exhibitions and bookshops and the unavoidable cafeteria which seems a crowning insensitivity in such a monument to extreme privation.

Birkenau – in Polish, Brzezinka – the second Auschwitz camp, is different. It is vast: murder's own cathedral. From the tower above the railway – too literally a terminus – the neat symmetry of its three hundred huts spreads out over more than four hundred acres, bounded by the wire fence that is punctuated with wooden turrets. It housed 100,000 at a time and killed more than a million. Like the turrets, some of the rotted huts have been rebuilt to give us 'the experience'. The rest are reduced to a plantation of brick chimneys, the result of rushed destruction as the Nazis fled.

There is, thankfully, little touristic exhibition. The camp is not even on the standard guided tour. As a result there is space to be alone, like the young Jew I saw walking slowly and methodically down the centre of the railway line, sleeper to sleeper, his eyes fixed on the ground. At key places, photographs, taken at that very spot when the camp was active, are mounted on posts – a cinematic flashback into the past. One photograph of unbearable poignancy is set near a copse and shows newly arrived mothers and children waiting nervously, perhaps not yet knowing the full meaning of the first 'selection'. We walk, conscious of the rustling witness of the trees.

Along the path is an unassuming, single-storey building. It is the reception centre to which these people would have come and experienced the finely calibrated demolition of their own selves: the handing over of all possessions, however cherished, the shaving of hair, the tattooing, the stripping naked, the showering.

Primo Levi again: "For the first time we became aware that our language lacks words to express this offence, the demolition of a man. In a moment, with almost prophetic intuition, the reality was revealed to us: we had reached the bottom. It is not possible to sink lower than this; no human condition is more miserable than this, nor could it conceivably be so. Nothing belongs to us any more; they have taken away our clothes, our shoes, even our hair; if we speak they will not listen to us, and if they listen they will not understand. They will even take away

16

our name: and if we want to keep it, we will have to find ourselves the strength to do so, to manage somehow so that behind the name something of us, of us as we were, still remains...

"Imagine now a man who is deprived of everyone he loves, and at the same time of his house, his habits, his clothes, in short, of everything he possesses: he will be a hollow man, reduced to suffering and needs, forgetful of dignity and restraint, for he who loses all often loses himself. He will be a man whose life and death can be lightly decided with no sense of human affinity, in the most fortunate of cases, on the basis of a pure judgment of utility. It is this way that one can understand the double sense of the word 'extermination camp' and it is now clear what we seek to express with the phrase: 'to lie on the bottom'."

One does not tread, even lightly, where victims of such extreme suffering have trod, so a glass pathway has been created that carries visitors a few inches above the floor, past the desks of clerks, the barber's area, and the autoclaves that disinfected the clothes. It is a place to experience that phrase – 'the banality of evil' – that was coined at the trial of Adolf Eichmann. Everywhere you see the mentality of clerks at work: the instinct to record, to list, to tabulate, to balance input and output – arrivals against cremations – to store, to re-use. A one-dimensional practicality with no moral overlay. But the building does contain a contrasting oasis of human feeling: a memorial room where survivors and their relatives have come to place photographs, flowers, messages and memories. It is full of love, though sometimes struggling with despair. One woman's poem reads:

How can I sing, my world is laid waste.
How can I play with wrung hands?
  Where are my dead, O God?
I see them in every dunghill, in every heap of ashes.
  O, tell me where you are.


Not far away are the four ruined crematoria, huge furnaces that worked round the clock every day for three years to wipe out a people. The ruins are untouched since the SS blew them up. Wild flowers are now pushing up around the nearby pool where the ashes were thrown.

So should we have gone? It is true that mass tourism can erode the solemnity or sanctity of such a place as surely as a legion of walkers can erode a mountain path. That may be happening at Auschwitz 1, though that, in turn, may save Birkenau from a similar fate. But the numbers will increase if Poland continues to prosper. A Jewish friend who has taken a conscious decision not to visit, told me he would like to see it pounded into the ground and grassed over under a simple monument. Despite misgivings, having been there I could not agree.

Auschwitz is a not a museum. It is the place where a too common anti-semitism flowed like globules of mercury to merge into one trembling weight, implicating us all. It is a still-threatening cloud in our mental climate. It is still powerfully present in the tension and conflicts of the modern world, as we are witnessing on a daily basis. Outside the Middle East, when considering Cambodia or Rwanda or Bosnia, or when ugly realpolitik insists on debating whether events in Darfur amount to genocide, we know that Auschwitz is the benchmark. There are some who, in the face of a mountain of direct and agonised testimony, still seek to deny that the 'Final Solution' ever took place, and some historians, like Deborah Lipstadt, worry that when the last survivors are gone 'denier' tendency might gain ground in the public mind. For survivors and their families it is a defining reality, for some an inescapable centre of their damaged lives. That is true for many of the groups who suffered there, but above all for Jews across the world. It is a memorial to man at his worst and the tomb of his victims. It is sacred ground.

For all those reasons it has to resist being sucked into the discourse of museums and 'experiences' and Disneyfication. It is no small danger. In a study of 'post war efforts to experience the Holocaust', *Fantasies of Witnessing*, its American author, Gary Weissman, tells how the children of survivors and those with no familial connection – 'non-witnesses' in Holocaust jargon – have a desperate urge to go beyond knowledge of the facts to "feel the Holocaust". He tells the tale of the son of a survivor of the Mathausen camp who visited the camp with his father. The son's wish and expectation was to be overwhelmed by the experience. Anything less would be a disappointment. But he was disappointed because he could not experience the horror his father knew. Weissman connects this common failure to experience the desired ecstasy of extreme emotion to a campaign during the 1990s to have one of the Birkenau crematoria rebuilt "so that they might 'better imagine' the horror". Rebuilding the barrack huts and the perimeter turrets and replacing some of the barbed wire was not enough for some. Only the reconstruction of a gas chamber would give people the requisite "slap in the face" that would ensure they did not forget. It would also, said the campaigners, be a way of fighting back against the Holocaust deniers.

Weissman shakes his head: "Imagining what life was like in the barracks requires some historical knowledge of the camps, whereas fantasising about dying in the gas chamber does not; this fantasy appeals to a sense of horror rather than a sense of history... If 'one of the best ways of ensuring that the Nazi atrocities are not forgotten is to reconstruct the gas chambers', what is being remembered by visitors who 'walk in'? How is imagining 'what the horror was like' related to not forgetting? What is not being forgotten?" Thankfully, the campaign came to nothing, but it is not difficult to see it being revived at some point in the future.

Such literalness devalues the human imagination, a process that, at the extreme, itself made Auschwitz possible. Museums, on the other hand, are places where art and architecture, artifice and metaphor are free to encourage that imagination. If 'feeling' is needed to deepen knowledge, nowhere is it better done than in Daniel Libeskind's Jewish Museum in Berlin. It is not a Holocaust Museum, but a museum that seeks to "integrate the tragic Jewish past with a future-oriented aesthetic asserting the vitality of Jewish life". Here, in the narrative exhibition, the Holocaust is, if anything, understated – not to diminish it but to establish an equally frightening continuity with the past and relevance to the present. It is intensely moving because it concentrates on the stories of individuals, refusing to make of Jews an impersonal group. But Libeskind has created two spaces in the building – two 'voids' – whose very emptiness is overwhelming. You enter one – the Holocaust Tower – through a metal door which is closed behind you. The high walls of smooth grey concrete rise from the triangular floor to a sharp point. Despite its height it is claustrophobic. The air is always chill. An open slit high up in the tower lets in the sound of the city. The sense of isolation and powerlessness is total. But the symbolism does not end there. Libeskind writes: "The voids of the museum provide a setting for nothing really to be displayed, because there is nothing really to be seen. It is just an emptiness that will never be eliminated from this city".

At Birkenau we boarded our minibus and did what so few did from that gate: departed. We passed the commandant's house, now, controversially, a Catholic Chaplaincy, a narrow road-width from the electric fence. In an evening sun the shadow of a turret might reach its door. Outside an open sports car, with a bouquet on its bonnet, awaited a bride and groom. We passed suburban houses and wondered what it was like to bring up a family, to eat meals and play and marry within sight of that fence. That night we dined in Krakow, a city where, before the war, 50,000 Jews lived. There are now no more than a few hundred. The old synagogue is locked. Another void.

## 3 January 2011

# Tangled campaigns

*Wales faced two referendums in 2011, within eight weeks of each other: a referendum on primary legislative powers for its National Assembly and a UK-wide referendum on the voting system.*

Spare a thought for Welsh politicians. Please. By the beginning of May 2011 they are going to be exhausted, broke and not a little confused after months of varying and probably reluctant cross party alliances, and none. The first four months of the year will entail non-stop campaigning, first in a referendum on 3 March on further law-making powers for the National Assembly, and then on 5 May another referendum on whether or not to introduce the Alternative Vote system for electing the Westminster Parliament, on the very same day as elections to the National Assembly – one straight party fight and two cross-party challenges that will divide the parties in different ways.

All four parties will officially support more powers for the Assembly, although there will undoubtedly be Labour and Tory splinter groups saying 'No'. True Wales – a 'No' grouping – will campaign under a name that ought to give the Advertising Standards Authority some concern. Labour will argue that the new powers are needed to fend off UK coalition plans, a line of argument that will push some Tories over the edge into opposition, while Lib Dems will deal with their embarrassment more quietly. A pull of *hiraeth* will mean that Neil Kinnock will probably toy with a '79 style intervention, unless loyalty to Ed Miliband prevails.

With only eight weeks to go, both sides are aware of how difficult it is to mobilise a political campaign in Wales, whatever the issue, but especially on one which is of no possible interest to the tabloid press. Do not forget *The Sun's* comprehensive coverage of the results of the 2007 Assembly elections – well, as comprehensive as you can get in thirteen words, yes, thirteen words, and those in a story devoted to the Scottish result – "Labour lost control of the Welsh Assembly as its devolution policy fell flat". The Welsh debate is going to be barely visible in the UK's twenty-four-hour news agenda. Catching the story there is going to be as difficult as catching a fish in a dead sea.

In the AV referendum, although some cross-party alliances may surface at a UK level, the concurrent Assembly elections in Wales will force parties to keep their distance from each other. Through an April campaign, Labour and Plaid, in coalition in Cardiff, will fight each other as well as the Conservatives and Lib Dems, whose partnership in the UK Government coalition will blunt their oppositional edge in Wales. The Welsh public will be expected to make sense of two football matches played on the same pitch at the same time by four teams who may turn up in different shirts in either half. If this were happening at a UK level the political sports correspondents would be adding some artificial frenzy to the confusion and demanding the abolition of the FA, but since the confusion will be confined to Wales and Scotland, they will probably leave it to the sketch writers.

Whatever the results of these votes, you can rest assured that the losing side or sides will be crying foul:

the winning margin's too narrow, or the turnout's too low; the voters could not understand the question; the media didn't pay enough attention; we were not allowed to get our ideas across; there was not enough information, there was too much of it, or it was biased. In fact, we are in a situation where it would be easier for campaigners to register their objections with the Electoral Commission well in advance. It would allow us all to 'move on' more quickly after the event. I offer some helpful suggestions.

No-one is happy with the date of the March referendum. It is perfectly possible that campaigners will be canvassing through February in the dark – clocks do not go forward until 27 March – though perhaps lightened by a deep covering of snow. Could differential turnout be affected by the presence or absence of gritter lorries in Cardiff, Gwynedd or Neath Port Talbot? In the past few weeks Cardiff gritters have rehearsed a stay indoors routine, and the staff of the Royal Mail have done likewise, presumably to measure how far they could disrupt the postal vote in the weeks before 3 March. Neither ploy seemed to worry the man who whizzed past our house in suburban Cardiff on cross-country skis, but I doubt if many will ski to the polls.

A quick thaw or just your increasingly average winter torrent may, of course, deliver floods, and it is difficult to envisage many determined democrats rowing to the polling booths to register their partiality for or dislike of Part 4 of the Government of Wales Act 2006. So might there be a possibility that the match will have to be postponed because of the weather, like Welsh rugby internationals in the days before covered stadia or underground heating? Does our Secretary of State, Cheryl Gillan,[2] have an alternative date in mind?

One option for her would be to postpone the Welsh referendum until the day of the Assembly elections and the AV referendum, to save money and maximise confusion. Since confusion in Wales and Scotland has not so far troubled her Deputy Prime Minister, who clearly does not think that tangled campaigns have any impact on voters once they have entered the polling booth, why should she worry? And I thought these were serious issues.

## 5 January 2011

## Another Welsh referendum

Coverage of the launch of the Yes campaign for the 3 March referendum on law-making powers for the National Assembly, illustrates perfectly what clumsy instruments referendums can be. Ostensibly, this is a referendum on the very arcane matter of whether to implement Part 4 of the Government of Wales Act 2006 – i.e to allow the National Assembly to pass laws on matters devolved to it, without a need to seek Westminster's permission on every single occasion.[3] But speeches and articles by both sides suggest that people want it to be about one of at least four things: the powers of the Assembly, the performance of the Assembly

---

[2] Cheryl Gillan MP, Secretary of State for Wales 2010-12
[3] It returned a big majority for legislative powers for Wales: 63% For, 36% Against

Government, Welsh influence in the UK and a test of national identity.

Professor Brian Morgan,[4] in particular, despite being in favour of giving law-making powers to the Assembly, wants the referendum debate to be about the performance of the Welsh Assembly Government. He takes issue with many of the Welsh Government's policies, as many of us might, but the problem with Professor Morgan's stance is that referendums do not allow you to say "Yes, but..." You have to say yes or no.

Why, in political debate in Wales, do we always confuse the performance of the Welsh Government with the powers of the institution, the National Assembly? Over my lifetime I can think of dozens of Westminster Government policies with which I disagreed: in the sixties the failure of the government to reform industrial relations; in the seventies the dog's dinner that was made of devolution legislation the first time round; in the eighties the closure of the coal industry, the approach to Europe and the poll tax; in the nineties the mess of the ERM and the building of the Millennium Dome; and in this last decade the failure to concentrate on Afghanistan rather than Iraq, the erosion of civil liberties, some daft ideas to spread casinos around the country, and even some dodgy decisions by the new UK coalition, such as to abolish the Food Standards Agency. I could also take issue, just as vehemently as Professor Morgan might, with the priority given by successive Governments to the finance industry to the point where it has screwed up all our futures for twenty years.

---

[4] Professor of Entrepreneurship, Cardiff Metropolitan University; previously Chief Economist at the Welsh Development Agency.

But I do not conclude from this catalogue of woe that Parliament should be constrained in its powers. On the contrary, what I would seek is greater clarity of responsibility, and in the case of devolution no confusion between different tiers: a clarity that enhances accountability, a clarity that does not consume time and attention in duplication of processes in Cardiff and London, a clarity that simplifies and increases public understanding. That is the main reason I will be voting Yes.

There are other reasons, too. Brian Morgan's complaints about particular policies do not tell the full story about the policy record and neither do they tell the whole story about devolution. But I am not going to get into the business of trading policy pluses and minuses, since that is a debate to be had between 3 March and the Assembly elections on 6 May. For the impact of the National Assembly is not to be measured solely by the workings of government, but also by the state of civil society. And civil society in Wales has been transformed in the last decade. Interest groups everywhere, particularly in the private and voluntary sectors, are more articulate, more savvy, more engaged with government about the needs of Wales and how they might be addressed. The world of business is much more attentive to policy than a decade ago. There is a greater sense of ownership of our own problems, a sense of responsibility for finding solutions rather than a freedom to whinge, even responsibility for our mistakes.

Today's Wales is not the Wales of 1979 or even 1997. It is now a bolder, less deferential place. That is why more and more are asking, as the Barry head-teacher did at the Yes launch – 'Not why would I, but why wouldn't I?' It is why more and more are asking why, in the ordering of devolution in Scotland, Wales and Northern Ireland, it should be thought that Welsh people are less deserving of responsibility than the Scots or the Northern Irish. Are we a lesser people than our Celtic cousins? Are we really less capable of ordering our society than Northern Ireland, a province half the size of Wales whose history of sectarian government begat forty years of civil strife, and where a sizeable part of the population actually want to live in a different state.

It is the Irish who have a phrase that captures the spirit of those who are now opposing a simple and rational extension of the National Assembly's legislative powers – 'Fuck the begrudgers'. The begrudgers wish to "always keep a-hold of nurse, for fear of finding something worse" is the surest way of preventing us from growing up and of reducing whatever small influence we have in these islands. Like many of my contemporaries I can recall vividly the way in which the 1979 'No' vote in the first devolution referendum destroyed Welsh influence for two decades. In the game of political poker we revealed that we had no cards, and pushed our chips back towards the Whitehall dealer. I doubt that Wales will want to do that again.

We would all like to see Wales increase its effectiveness at home and its influence and leverage within the UK. Influence depends on respect, respect responds to self-respect, self-respect requires you to take responsibility. I shall be voting for responsibility on 3 March, and debate policy only when the deed is done.

11 December 2011

## Europe's awkward squad

*The December 2011 summit in Brussels tried to deal with the effects of the 2007-08 crash on the EU and the Euro. David Cameron found himself isolated.*

European summits are often over-dramatised by the UK's press: the implication of a superlative in the very word 'summit', the ceremonial greeting of heads of state, the motorcades, the tension of negotiation, deals done at the dead of night by tired ministers and officials, usually the last minute resolution of the seemingly irreconcilable, followed by spinning press conferences. But it would be hard to level the charge of over-dramatisation on this occasion. At stake was the future of the world economy, and, potentially, the most radical peaceful change in the governance of Europe since the collapse of the Holy Roman Empire. And it would be hard not to be intensely disappointed at the outcome, on no less than four counts:

First, the continued lack of decisive steps to shore up the continent's finances in the short term, including Germany's continued unwillingness to allow full-scale intervention by the European Central Bank, and the bank's own agreement with that line. Second, the absence of a plan to encourage economic growth across Europe, to accompany greater rigour in the management of national finance. Third, the prospect of new tougher rules for eurozone countries that will make it very difficult to provide such a growth stimulus in future. Fourth, Britain's obvious and total isolation, on grounds – defence of the

City of London – that look straightforward but are more flimsy the more they are examined.

Such reasons for gloom are only compounded by the smug pleasure of euro-sceptic politicians and press, and the dispirited reaction of those who have supported the European project. The former salivate at the prospect of the UK's departure from Europe, the latter bite their nails as they worry that the departure is now more possible. It is understandable that some of our exasperated European partners should breathe a sigh of relief at the prospect of seeing their difficult neighbour pack up and go. For too long we have been Europe's awkward squad. In the circumstances, we should not be surprised that the service upon the UK – self-service is more accurate – of a kind of national ASBO might seem, to many, to be overdue.

As Nye Bevan said at the thought of a Labour conference contriving to send a British Foreign Secretary 'naked into the conference chamber': "And you call that statesmanship. I call it an emotional spasm." What would he have said if the Foreign Secretary was left outside the door?

David Cameron's battle was lost long before he reached Brussels. As was pointed out at a recent conference in Cardiff, countries that want the empathy of others in moments of difficulty have to build up a credit balance in the good times – a kind of Keynesianism of manners rather than money. But instead the Prime Minister has both abandoned potential mainstream allies in European centre-right parties, and preferred to lecture the eurozone from a distance. Yet what right have we to do so? A country that sees 'muddling through' as a virtue, and thinks intellectual coherence in public affairs an alien continental habit, is hardly in a position to criticise the rest of Europe for insufficient rigour in thinking through the Euro issue. A country that, notwithstanding devolution, has embodied a mindset more centralised even than France, is hardly in a position to lecture other countries on the virtues of subsidiarity and self-determination.

In all our time in, first, the EEC and then the EU we have given the impression of being reluctant members of the club. Harold Wilson and James Callaghan were the first to attempt renegotiation, in order to justify a referendum that would salve Labour's divisions. Margaret Thatcher was even more bullish, but successful, in renegotiation, while giving succour later to the eurosceptics in her own party who attempted to skewer John Major. Even David Cameron this weekend has spoken about 'the bits of Europe that suit Britain', as if this were an *a la carte* restaurant, preferably serving very small portions.

In his magisterial survey of Britain's relationship with Europe – *This Blessed Plot*[5] – the late Hugo Young contrasted the post-war makers of the new Europe, who saw their creation as a triumph, with a very different British mindset.

"For Britain, by contrast, the entry into Europe was a defeat: a fate she had resisted, a necessity reluctantly accepted, the last resort of a once great power, never for one moment a climactic or triumphant engagement with the construction of Europe. This has been integral in the national psyche, perhaps only half articulated since 1973. The sense

---

[5] p2, *This Blessed Plot,* by Hugo Young. Macmillan 1998.

of the Community as a place of British failure –
proof of Britain's failed independence, site of her
failed domination..."

And this mentality has been nurtured, often
mendaciously, by large sections of the press who have
sustained a barrage of emotional criticism of European
institutions, with a constant implication of British
superiority. They have polluted a legitimate debate. Only
a few weeks ago, at an Institute of Welsh Affairs
conference on regeneration, a questioner from the floor
bemoaned the inability of some local firms to win
contracts, casually blaming it all on Brussels, as if this
were an incontrovertible truth. Expert speakers on the
panel reminded him that the problem lay as much with
the actions of Welsh civil servants and their legal advisers
as with anything emanating from the EU.

Beyond Wales the little Englander mentality in full
spate is not a pretty sight. It is backward looking. It is
often as much anti-government as anti-Europe, a rejection
of European social democracy. It is a distorted view of
the world and a distorted view of the UK's clout within
it. Even financial commentators are recognising that the
British veto has not even guaranteed the very security for
the City of London that it was designed to achieve.

Of course, the institutions of the EU are far from perfect
– as are our own. Neil Kinnock, when a EU commissioner,
struggled hard for internal reform, but had to leave much
unfinished business. But these shortcomings, like those of
any human institution, do not necessarily undermine the
fundamental arguments for the EU's existence: a guarantor
of European peace, an immense single market that

contributes to growth, European-wide regulation that levels playing fields and helps both consumers and citizens, a necessary pooling of sovereignty that allows us to be more effective in a globalised world.

These powerful fundamentals will still be valid arguments for close European cooperation in Europe whether the Euro survives or not. The potential for calamity is dangerously large. Wales, at the wrong end of economic league tables, has powerful additional reasons for wanting the understanding of Europe. It will be interesting to see how the report of Parliament's Welsh Affairs Committee inquiry into inward investment takes account of our new situation. In Scotland it will be surprising if Alex Salmond does not find a way of playing the debacle to his advantage. The consequences of the last few days are unpredictable, both for the seventeen countries in the eurozone and all twenty-seven members of the EU. Whatever happens Britain must remain at the conference table. We will still need empathic European friends, not merely disillusioned colleagues. We will still need to be influential and to be seen to be influential in Europe by the rest of the world. Otherwise every country of the UK is diminished.

30 December 2011

## Vision of a European republic

*A new book on Europe was a reminder that the UK rarely plugs into debates about the future of the continent. Too often we have been spectators rather then engaged participants.*

33

Europe has had rather too many inglorious moments in the recent past – indecision on the Balkans, division on Iraq, prevarication on the Euro – and few will bet that European leaders will snatch victory from the jaws of defeat when they meet at the end of this month to search once again for economic salvation. In a new book[6] David Marquand argues that they are paying the price of decades of avoidance of fundamental issues, issues where Europe's past and future meet.

David Marquand is one of the most astute historians of our recent politics. His history of twentieth century British politics, *Britain since 1918*, published three years ago and sub-titled *The strange career of British democracy* was a refreshing analysis that got away from the clichéd categorisation of our politics as 'left' or 'right'. His monograph, *Decline of the public*, was a chilling reminder of the way in which a combination of the market and party politics have eroded that public space between the two that is so essential for a living, engaged democracy.

Now in *The End of the West: The once and future Europe*, he has turned his attention to a cause that he has served both in British politics – as an MP and commentator – and beyond, as an official in the European Commission. In intensely readable and pacy prose, he does not hide or resile from his pro-Europe convictions, but rather believes that the only way to champion Europe is to face it with very difficult questions that it has so far preferred to avoid. These questions arise from the rebirth of ethnic communities below the level of the nation state, the rise of xenophobic populism, and the democratic

---

[6] *The End of the West: The once and future Europe*, by David Marquand. Princeton University Press. 2011.

deficit in Europe's governance. Philosophic debate about the nature of Europe also poses questions about the proper limits of its expanding boundaries.

He applauds the 'astonishing success' of the unique European experiment in supranational government – 'the longest period of peace and prosperity in post-Roman European history', old enemies learning to live together, an economy second only to the United States, the spread of guaranteed human rights and the rule of law, the abolition of the death penalty in all member states, the adoption (albeit with considerable variations) of a European social model, the enlargement of Europe to embrace the formerly Communist countries of Eastern Europe.

And, again, in a more easily visible form: French football players playing for British teams (and he might have added Welsh rugby players playing for French teams), the *Financial Times* becoming a continental as well as British newspaper, European lorries thundering across borders, the 'Bologna process' making European university qualifications interchangeable, and 1.2 million students having participated in the Erasmus programme for student exchanges.

But for all this, he sees Europe as a 'hobbled giant', increasingly paralysed by 'a fatal disconnect dividing the peoples of Europe from the European elites' and ill-equipped to face up to new challenges. He asks:

"Can [Europe] overcome its internal contradictions – between European elites and their people, between democratic promise and technocratic reality? Can it develop institutions with the legitimacy, will and capacity to enable it to join the United States,

China and India as a global power? Or is it doomed to remain an economic giant and a political pygmy – rich, fat, vulnerable and increasingly irrelevant to the new world that is taking shape beyond its frontiers?"

Next week EU governments – whether seventeen, twenty-seven or twenty-eight of them is not clear – will grapple with some of these questions in a bid to save the Eurozone. Marquand's contention is that Europe is facing these questions in an atmosphere of acute crisis because of the technocratic way in which the European Union has evolved – an avowedly political union, according to its founders, but one where 'integration would be a cumulative process spreading, like an inkblot, from one policy area to the next', and obviating the need to 'debate the nature of the final step or to chart the likely course of its arrival'. The Community's politics, he says, were 'ostentatiously undramatic', 'its processes opaque and, for most Europeans, mind-numbingly tedious... the politics of the conference table and the *couloir*, not of the debating chamber or the election meeting'.

"The vision they embodied was of Europe as a vast shopping mall, dedicated to an ideal of bourgeois contentment and ever-advancing prosperity. It was a vision for the boom of the 1990s and 2000s. Whether it will suffice for the bust is not so clear."

European leaders will find their talks in the coming weeks terribly uncomfortable not only because of the hardship that a group commitment to yet more austerity will impose on their own peoples, but also because they have neglected to take their electorates with them and to build a sense of European solidarity, leaving European institutions with deficits in legitimacy just as large as the financial deficits of most member states. This is why Marquand sees monetary union as 'the last stop on the old road, not the first step on the new one'.

This, he says, is the revenge of politics on the narrowly economic focus of the EU's development.

"Its institutions cannot mobilise consent because they are not rooted in consent; because they can't mobilise consent they can't lead the union into the high-political sphere and overcome the threat of global irrelevance."

Some of these criticisms could have been, and have been voiced by Euro-sceptics, but he comes to a very different conclusion. He argues that if Europe is to retain a global relevance in tackling the daunting agenda of "climate change, energy shortages, the desperate poverty of the world's 'bottom billion', international terrorism and, above all, the waning of the west" it will need a leap of imagination comparable to that of the founding fathers of the United States 220 years ago, in order to get out of 'the No Man's Land between confederalism and federalism', the 'stultifying compromise' in which it is currently trapped.

He does not flinch from federalism – although the light-touch federalism of Switzerland is more to his taste than that of Germany – but he anticipates the charge of utopian idealism, as well as specific objections. To the charge that Europe is too diverse for federalism, that you cannot create a European democracy in the absence of a deeper sense of European citizenship – a European *demos* – he cites the USA and India as countries where 'the *demos* was made by democracy, not democracy by the *demos*'. That said, he believes the first job should be the encouragement of a European public realm through direct elections to the European presidency and through union-wide referenda on the admission of new members.

He dismisses, perhaps rather too easily, the fear of 'a superstate crashing through the walls of nationhood', arguing that federalism is of its essence decentralist. That is true in a formal sense, but it has not stopped federal governments in the USA and Germany from gradually accruing greater powers. But like his fellow historian, Norman Davies – whose recent book[7] *Vanished Kingdoms: The history of half-forgotten Europe*, is a magnificent and compendious reminder of the transient nature of states and empires – Marquand is not a believer in the immutability of the present nation states, or in their present efficacy. Is it an accident that both Marquand and Davies have connections with Wales, indeed the dedication in Davies's book is in Welsh – *I'r Anghofiedig* (To the unremembered).

Faced with pressure from the rebirth of older identities from below and Europeanisation and globalisation from above, he says:

"The humbled, weakened, pressured and often be-wildered European states of the twenty-first century

---

[7] *Vanished Kingdoms: the history of half-forgotten Europe*, by Norman Davies. Allen Lane. 2011.

have become more, not less, anxious to cling to the prerogatives that remain to them... They are, in short, in denial; and as people in denial often do, they become tense, rigid, deceitful, and irrationally defensive."

This book will prompt much debate, but that is Marquand's point: that what has been lacking is a debate, but not a debate on Europe framed by the zero-sum mentality of defensive nation-states, but rather a wider and deeper European conversation about Europe's meaning, mission and purpose and the means to fulfil them. His is a broad and tolerant vision of a European republic that even he admits may still be some way off. Let us hope that such a debate does not have to take place only in the wake of another catastrophe.

## 27 April 2014

## Confession of a prejudiced pro-European

*Transactional arguments were not enough to stop the onward March of UKIP*

The debate on Europe has ceased to be a reasoned debate, it seems more of a visceral struggle between deep-seated attitudes – prejudices if you like. So, if you don't like UKIP's prejudices, especially those of some of its candidates, try mine.

First, I am deeply prejudiced in favour of peace, and in favour of any institutions that make war less likely.

The EEC and the EU have been spectacularly successful in creating, not just an absence of war, but a meaningful peace, in which people have been able to grow together. The process goes on.

One day in the 1980s, on a train between Paddington and Cardiff, the broadcaster, Wynford Vaughan Thomas, told me of wonderful journeys through Eastern Europe that he had undertaken as a young man in the 1930s. He then dug out a sheet of paper from his bag and, with a fountain pen, drew a remarkably accurate and rather beautiful map of Europe – from John O'Groats to Istanbul – before plotting his youthful journey. "It's incredible to think that half that map has been off limits to me for decades," he said, and he was right. He had reported from bombers over Berlin. He had advanced with allied troops through Italy. He had been into Belsen. The Iron Curtain offended him. He did not live to see it fall. If he had he would have raised a glass of very fine wine.

Anyone watching events in the Ukraine today, will realise how easily countries can fall into war. Echoes of Sarajevo in 1914. A miscalculation here, a misunderstanding there. Overt power, opaque motives. Local passions, continental consequences. A stable and peaceful Europe needs its institutions, however imperfect they may be.

Second, I am an unashamed pro-European, instinctively so. I had known it for a long time: the effect of Latin and French at school, boyhood hitch-hiking, history at college. My family and I have enjoyed and learned from the open continent. I even helped draft some sympathetic information leaflets during the 1975 referendum on Europe. But in 1997 I updated and refreshed my prejudice during six weeks away from Europe at a business school in Philadelphia. I was in a group of forty people drawn from different industries from around the world. We were taught by some of the brightest brains around, but some of the lecturers were clearly proponents of fashionable neo-liberal theories that, a decade later, would lead to a financial catastrophe, the economic and social effects of which of our continent is still living through. They were adamant that the European social model was doomed. Only the American liberal model would work, they argued, urging us to follow the example of Asian countries, although some Asian currencies were crashing even as they spoke.

This led to fierce arguments between we Europeans and our American friends. If it was a choice between the American or European models, I knew instinctively which side I was on. I might not want to go the whole hog to a rather conformist Scandinavian solution, but I know – as most of us do – that libelling social solidarity as the next best thing to Soviet communism is barking mad. It ends up with a Democratic President being demonised for trying to secure even a minimal degree of health insurance for fifty million of his people who had no safety net. I dislike the harsh instincts that lie behind America's ultra right wing Tea Party, and extend that dislike to those in this country who would push us in the same direction – towards ever smaller government and the diminishment of the public realm. Their victory would change the nature of my country more radically than any impact they allege from immigration.

Third, I am unshakeably prejudiced against those who propagate the big lie. This is the only description that one can attach to Mr Farage's poster campaign: "26 million people in Europe are looking for work. And whose jobs are they after?" It is a brazen and calculated deception. It is the technique perfected by Josef Goebbels. Make the lie big enough and you put it beyond the possibility of proof. Create fear and suspicion, and a lot of people will look over their shoulder. It is not difficult to do, especially when people everywhere are already unsettled by the pace of change, by technologies that make their long learnt skills redundant, or global industries that can shift production to wherever in the world they can find the cheapest labour. Simplistic explanations are always easier to sell than complex ones, and never carry a health warning. These fundamental uncertainties are, unfortunately, endemic. That is why Mr Farage – whose name is pronounced with a surprisingly French inflection – is not alone. He has his counterparts in almost every country, not all of whom exude his own back bar bonhomie. History, as well as our daily news, tells us that thuggery of the deed is not far behind the disguised thuggery of the word.

Lastly, I am prejudiced against shifting the blame for our own sins of omission or commission onto others. That is what people do when they claim that the EU is the problem, rather than part of the solution. The EU gets the blame for all kinds of restrictions, when for years it has been the 'gold-plating' of EU directives by British civil servants that has been to blame. The present UK government has been trying to prevent its own officials doing this – in the process proving the point. If the EU is the problem, why have other member states been more effective in safeguarding ownership of their own key industries than ourselves? The beam is in our own eye.

There are plenty of things in the institutions of the EU that need reform, but in order to make the EU work better, rather than to protect the UK from some non-existent existential threat. After all, our own British institutions are hardly flawless conceptions. But it's a pity that a constructive engagement with refining our continental tier of governance, will be drowned out in the next few weeks, by Mr Farage's display of narcissistic insecurities.

## 8 September 2014

# Wales needs its own Plan B

*Many in Britain held their breath as we approached the referendum on Scottish independence. A Yes vote would have had consequences for Wales too.*

The panic may be necessary, but panic it is. With polls saying the Scottish referendum is too close to call, in the next few days Scotland will be offered, constitutionally, something just short of the earth, while markets and big industries will apply the economic frighteners. Meanwhile the Queen will be wondering whether her reign will be known not for its longevity but for being the last over a united kingdom, and whether the annual trip to Balmoral will henceforth be a trip abroad.

How did we get to this precipice? It is easy to blame poor tactics on the part of the present UK government, but it is more deep-rooted than that. History and the asymmetry of the United Kingdom make it inherently difficult for Whitehall to heed consistently even the periphery of England itself. A centralising mindset, almost unmatched in Europe, has survived devolution to Scotland and Wales. Centralisation of government and business, the emasculation of local government, the primacy of finance, the neglect of the productive economy, the excessive lauding of the market, the undermining of social solidarity have all made their contribution. Margaret Thatcher had no Plan B for the coal-mining communities.

But what will be the consequences if Scotland does not resist the urge to push us all over the edge? There is much general talk to the effect that there will be change, whatever Scotland decides. No doubt, but a Yes vote will not produce the same kind of change as a No vote. And it might not be as benign. A bare majority for No could well force the kind of full-scale constitutional reassessment of the governance of the UK that is decades overdue. The First Minister of Wales, Carwyn Jones, has been campaigning for a UK Constitutional Convention to do just that for at least eighteen months, unfortunately with precious little response until now. I say 'could' because the British penchant for fudging constitutional issues is very deep-seated. That is why we still have the absurdity of hereditary peers in the House of Lords. But Britain has now run out of excuses.

The consequences of a Yes vote are of a different order, and far less predictable. It is difficult to overestimate the impact of Scottish secession from the union. Yes, we can have fun contemplating a name for the rump UK – Little Britain or, more controversially, England. Don't laugh, the elephant next door would comprise ninety-two per cent of the population. We can amuse ourselves re-designing the Union Jack to remove the Scottish saltire and insert a dragon or the cross of St David. We can debate whether a Yes vote would require David Cameron's resignation, or whether Boris Johnson might become the first Prime Minister of 'England plus' on the basis that he might provide England with a psychological pick me up. But beneath all this would be the reality that the loss of Scotland would be more traumatic for England – and particularly for the political, financial and cultural elites of the south east – than the loss of the British empire. We cannot know what the psychological effect of such an amputation will be.

There is a common but false assumption that the United Kingdom has endured for all time. Wales was annexed in the 16th century, the crowns of England and Scotland came together under the Stuarts at the beginning of the 17th century, union with Scotland followed at the start of the 18th century and union with Ireland in the 19th century. The loss of empire was swifter, but took the best part of a century. Irish Home rule was debated and fought for from the 1870s to 1921 when it was achieved. In 1931 the Statute of Westminster declared that colonial legislatures were no longer subservient to the Imperial Parliament. India won its independence in 1947, ninety years after the first Indian mutiny. In 1956 the Suez crisis exposed our lingering imperial pretensions. And four years later Harold Macmillan reminded an audience in South Africa of the 'winds of change' blowing through the continent. Importantly, as the empire ebbed away the power elites were able to suck on two comfort blankets: first, the fact of having been the victor in 1945;

second, membership of what was then a very small nuclear club. The UK's status was not dependent on land mass, population, natural resources or finance. After all, at the end of the war we were broke.

Scottish secession would be a different matter. In historical terms it would have come remarkably swiftly, and the comfort blankets are threadbare. 1945 is now too far away, the world's nuclear club is bigger, and our nuclear deterrent seems less relevant to modern circumstances and is, at least partly, American. On the other hand, population and economic performance are now a significant determinant of our relationship with Europe. They help determine our financial contribution and rebate, and our influence over allocation of portfolios in the Commission. The UK's population determines the number of our seats in the European Parliament. Our military capacity affects our standing in NATO and the UN, as well as our relationship with the United States.

All these would be affected by Scottish secession. It will not be possible – as it was with the loss of empire – for the power elites to go on pretending that nothing had changed. England (and London in particular) would feel this diminishment far more than Wales. The effects of trauma are not always predictable, and recent polling on English attitudes provides no comfort.

Wales would face perils of its own. With Scotland gone, we might find it easier to get a better overall funding deal through reform of the Barnett formula. But other consequences might be harsher and more unpredictable. For instance, although Scotland would no longer be part of UKTI's inward investment team, it would be fighting its own corner – like Ireland – probably with a sharply reduced corporation tax. Toughest of all would be that Wales would be faced with the harsh reality of its own lack of leverage. The threat of independence for Wales has no current credibility. We do not have oil. Neither do we have – like Northern Ireland – a border with another state that has a claim on us. Faced with this situation, over the last half century we have been very adept at using Scotland as the battering ram, and following in its wake – what one BBC colleague called 'kiltstreaming'. That option would be gone. The only leverage that we could build would have to be on the foundation of superior performance that, regrettably, still seems a long way off. We have a fair idea of what Wales might want out of a new UK settlement in the event of a Scottish No vote. There are no signs yet that we have a Welsh contingency plan in the event of a Yes vote. We need one urgently.

## 19 September 2014

## Scotland – and England

*The result of the Scottish referendum still left England nursing a grievance.*

The febrile atmosphere of the last days of the Scottish referendum seems not to have abated. The panic induced by the one opinion poll that, the weekend before polling, put Yes voters in the lead, quickly infected a large part of the London-based press. The infection still lingers in this immediate post-referendum period – demonstrating rather forcefully once again, how English rather than British a press it is. Given, too, the press's right wing mindset, the hysteria has been exacerbated by the knowledge that English grievance, such as it is, can be turned into a stick with which to beat the left, and Ed Miliband in particular: how dare he prevaricate when England stands in such mortal danger.

The post-referendum jostling began with David Cameron's Friday morning statement. It was delivered with his familiar cadences of urgency – one of his favourite tropes. You could almost see him reaching for his cuffs to roll up his sleeves. But the situation demanded more than theatre. The awful truth is, as Carwyn Jones said, the British establishment almost lost Scotland. The lookouts on the watchtower had either been asleep or awake but unseeing. That in itself requires some explanation and introspection. The explanation lies in dominant modes of thinking in the centres of British power.

First, the establishment view of the British constitution has been expressed down the years in an endless plain chant of hubristic self-satisfaction that leads inexorably to an instinct to defer reform until the last minute. Pragmatism, procrastination and muddling through have been elevated to cardinal virtues, immortalised in that Sir Humphrey-like phrase, 'there are times when one must rise above principle.' Principles are regarded as rather dangerous, and probably French. As Professor Peter Hennessey put it in his pre-devolution book, *Muddling Through,* "One of the cardinal rules of the British way of government is that panic must always be portrayed as poise, and desperate improvisation as the pragmatic product of centuries of wisdom and experience."

Second, a substantial part of the governing elite – despite ostensibly defending 'the union' – paradoxically, in the depth of their souls have never seen the country as a union, but rather as a single unitary state, and devolution a rather unfortunate aberration. Tony Blair did not believe in it, but was persuaded to proceed as an act of piety following the death of his predecessor as party leader, John Smith. Westminster and Whitehall never liked, or perhaps even understood, the change in the nature of the state that was implicit in the creation of the devolved administrations. The people who bestowed federal systems on Canada and Australia and, irony of ironies, on Germany after the war, could not bring themselves to contemplate anything similar for the United Kingdom. Until now. That in itself is a measure of the Scottish earthquake.

Third, as the author David Goodhart, has commented, "The English remain semi-literate in the language of modern identity." England may be coming up the learning curve, but it has some way to go.

These factors explain why so many approaches to constitutional change by those in power seem strangely incomplete and ill thought through. David Cameron's morning-after statement fell into both these categories. No consultation with the devolved administrations, the problem stated only as one involving discrete issues in four separate territories – four-country rhetoric, but two-country action that morning: Scotland and England. No hint of a means to bring consistency and coherence to the whole. Neither did he point to any connection to the wider aspects of the constitution – the Commons, the Lords, electoral reform, the empowerment of local government or any other means to the renewal of our democracy – or to any possible foundation of principle. No. Any repairs to the battered British constitution were to be limited, and despatched with all the speed of the Dangerous Dogs Act.

None of this should come as a surprise. Wider movements for constitutional change in this country have always found themselves struggling up a very long and steep hill – a Sisyphean journey. The extension of the franchise to full suffrage took ninety-six years – from 1832 to 1928. More recently, the Charter 88 movement in the late 1980s, the Power Inquiry a decade ago, and the campaigns of the Electoral Reform Society, have mostly run into the sand. The reform of the House of Lords has been obstructed for more than one hundred years – that is how effective English or British conservatism (small 'c') can be.

Given this dilatory record, what is it that explains today's rush? The desire to keep one's vow to Scotland is understandable, even if that vow was cobbled and pledged with undue haste. But the notion that the English suburbs and countryside are aflame with a resentment that brooks no compromise or delay is scarcely believable. Yes, many English people are now prioritising their English identity over British. Yes, many English people (and not a few Welsh) are irritated that the Scots have had such an unwarranted good deal out of the Barnett formula. But I doubt that the general population are exercised by the West Lothian question quite as much as English Conservative MPs and UKIP candidates.

One has to ask how much of this anger is

manufactured? After all, the notion that the British constitution, taken as a whole, is somehow grossly unfair to England, or that England has not done well out of the union beggars belief. England is a nation with eighty-four per cent of the population of the UK, eighty-two per cent of elected members in the Westminster Parliament, and a similar percentage of its peers. England dominates the Whitehall machine. Even quoting expenditure per head figures for the four countries is usually confined to identifiable expenditure on functions that, outside England, are devolved. The figures leave out of account things like the distribution of defence expenditure and research spending – such as that by Vince Cable's Technology Strategy Board not to mention things such as the Olympic Games. There is still some doubt as to whether Scotland, Wales and Northern Ireland, will benefit from any payment of Barnett consequentials in respect of HS2 that is planned to cost £43bn. Meanwhile Wales has to haggle with the UK Treasury over the electrification of the Valleys Lines. All this without considering other examples of dominant non-governmental English influence, such as the financial system, or our press and broadcasting institutions, or even arts philanthropy where more than eighty per cent of all arts philanthropy goes into central London. The truth is that even devolution scarcely dents English influence. That is the reality of co-habiting with an elephant. And from England's point of view London is a bigger problem than Scotland.

Moreover, none of the solutions posed to the West Lothian question are without their problems for England as much as for any other country in the UK. English votes for English Laws (EVEL) attempts to get round the problem of differing party majorities in the UK and in England, but they also raise questions about Cabinet responsibility as well as the role and composition of the House of Lords. The same might not be true of an English Parliament separate from a UK Parliament, as long as England was content with a unicameral legislature. But even that solution forces us to consider the political dynamics of the co-existence of UK and English Parliaments and governments. Surprisingly, in this context, the division of power between Yeltsin and Gorbachev in the last days of the USSR has been mentioned warmly by some commentators. Some precedent! The tension between the English Boris and the current Prime Minister might be of a different order if Boris J. ran England and not only London.

This is not to argue against either EVEL or an English Parliament, but merely to confirm that these are issues that need more care and study than can be achieved before next year's general election. Carwyn Jones has been right all along in calling for a UK Constitutional Convention. But England, too, needs to have an internal debate, especially at a time when its own internal dynamics are in flux. Strange that the gradualism that England has always lauded, is now intolerable for some.

8 January 2015

## Death of satire

Yesterday I sat in my car outside B&Q – I needed a plug for the sink – for a full half hour listening to the news from

Paris that twelve people have been shot in the offices of the satirical magazine, *Charlie Hebdo*. It's appalling and frightening. I just wish it were unbelievable, but there is too much evidence that the world has gone mad. I could feel my eyes prickling. I was trying to imagine the startled, disbelieving faces of the group as masked gunmen burst into their editorial meeting. They would have been discussing the next issue. Did this or that article hit the right target? Was it funny? Had they just shared a new joke? Did the gunmen burst in on banter and laughter? These people were cartoonists, for God's sake, two of them pushing eighty. Were they grandfathers? I wonder. If they were, I would bet they had drawn funny birthday cards for their children and grandchildren, or nieces and nephews. They would have been popular, loved.

More difficult to imagine the gunmen, anonymous in their black garb. All human feeling cauterised, all perspective lost. Bloodlust or imagined offence – which the chicken, which the egg? Converts or psychopaths? Hooliganism or religion, either or both gone rancid. If the former, what warped their young lives? If the latter, when and how did they fall for far too simple answers to life and death? Evan Davies introduced *Newsnight* last night, choking with emotion. Place de la Concorde full of people holding up makeshift banners saying, "Je suis Charlie". Deeply moving.

This morning's papers are full of the massacre, but none of them are carrying the cartoons that made *Charlie Hebdo* a target, unlike papers in some other European countries. The jihadists know that most of the time fear works.

But an impressive turnout of religious leaders in Paris – Christian, Jewish, Muslim, even a Buddhist. This must be causing immense pain to the Muslim community, and not just fear of a backlash. The vast majority of Muslims will be as horrified as anyone else, not just because they can feel the horror of it, but also because such actions do immense damage to Muslims and to their faith. The jihadist ideology is undoubtedly a perversion of Islam, but the question for Muslims must be, how to fight back. For the real answer to the jihadists must come from within the global Islamic community. Why aren't there more signs of resistance? Is it structural?

At a local level many individual Muslim leaders have been unequivocal in their condemnation of the killings, emphasising that there is no Koranic justification for them – quite the contrary – even if depictions of Mohammed are offensive to believers. But at the same time there is no sense of a concerted international Muslim movement to put these murderers beyond the pale. Is that because organisationally Islam is a loose network – no developed authority or hierarchy, no bishops let alone Popes? Is the lack of a world Islamic summit, a kind of Muslim Lambeth conference, to condemn the gun simply a sign of organisational deficiency, or because it would risk revealing more division than consensus. Will Sunnis and Shias ever see eye to eye?

# BATTLE STATIONS

3 July 2015

## Europe means us

Within the next two years the United Kingdom is promised "an In/Out referendum" on our membership of the European Union. A sharp binary choice. It will decide the future of our country's most important international involvement – a relationship that, at the time of the vote, will be nearly forty-five years old. It is a relationship that impacts every single citizen. Those who would end this relationship ask us to put our faith in an angry fistful of myths.

The first is that our kingdom's watery boundary creates an ineradicable distinction between us and our continental brothers and sisters; that we ourselves, and our problems and issues, are different and separate; that we can stand aloof from our neighbours. This has never been true. For centuries we were part of the Roman Empire. For a millennium we were fully part of Catholic Europe. Our Protestantism was derived from elsewhere in northern Europe. An instinct for standing aloof has not prevented us from being drawn into wars with Spain, France, Italy and Germany. In the twentieth century we were not able to stand aside from Europe's two civil wars, the bloodiest in history. For the last half century the European Union has preserved an unprecedented internal peace by focusing on our common interests and weaving common solutions. We secured Europe from external threat through a similar joint effort in NATO. In the process we extended democracy to millions. As war reappears in too many places and terrorism spreads its bloody tentacles, that common effort is surely more necessary than ever.

The second myth is that we would be better able to face the world's other problems on our own. The plagues of the middle ages did not respect borders, neither do the plagues of today: crime and the trafficking of people, drugs and arms, terrorism, the pollution of air and sea. Does anyone believe that these problems, or the problems of migration and climate change, can be better addressed by our standing outside the European tent?

A third myth is that the European Union is a burdensome imposition on British citizens. That is not true for us in Wales who benefit so much from the EU's regional policies. It is not true for the thousands of UK citizens who work for overseas companies seeking a space within the European market. Neither is it true for Britain's farmers or exporters, those that enjoy protection at work, consumers who want safe products, families that enjoy our newly clean rivers and beaches, or who, through cheap air travel, have become the most travelled generations in history.

A fourth myth is that we can be as influential outside the EU as within it. In a globalised world, where the wealth and power of corporations often exceeds those of quite prosperous countries, and continental powerhouses such as the US, China and India sit at the conference table, do we wish to be an effective and influential player in a weighty European team, or a small country tugging at the coat-tails of the great powers, committed to abiding by rules we will not have helped shape?

Some would sacrifice all this in the name of sovereignty. But sovereignty is not a free-standing icon, it is Russian Doll. Different sovereignties lay the one within the other, from the very local to the continental. That arrangement reflects the complexity of the modern world. Untrammelled sovereignty is a myth, shared power is real power. We must share it and use it within a Europe that belongs to us all.

## 5 August 2015

## Through Europe to the world

*A visit to a German car museum is a chastening experience.*

As David Cameron courts Angela Merkel in his quest for release from the rack of Euro-sceptic torture, he does so as supplicant. She responds as the leader of a nation that long ago supplanted the UK as the workshop of the world and is now the dominant force in Europe. Her view will decide Cameron's fate as surely as it has decided the fate of Greece.

The UK prides itself on the strength of its financial sector and on its creative industries yet, unlike Germany, it has been astonishingly careless of its capacity for making things, exporting things and, even more inexplicably, owning things. Recently these ironies were brought home to me forcefully at BMW's huge exhibition centre near the Olympic Park in Munich – BMW Welt (BMW World). The car company dominates this city, supporting everything from Bayern Munich football to the Bavarian State Opera. BMW Welt – part company museum, part showroom, part exercise in corporate pride (or is it aggrandisement?) – is a series of somewhat overblown silver palaces that, appropriately, bridge a motorway. Inevitably, they generate conflicting responses: the place is superbly designed and presented, but any celebration of the car these days, however well crafted, must jar with one's consciousness of the environmental damage that the car has done and is doing. Some will see no conflict, the verdict conclusively against the automobile.

And yet. The BMW Welt museum tells a tale – brilliantly, and with little expense spared – about a century of extraordinary engineering innovation that conveys many unspoken messages: about human creativity and an unending quest for improvement, about the symbiotic relationship between beauty and engineering, about the relationship between military and civil demands, and about the economic benefits of particular models of corporate ownership. It would be a folly to dismiss it as a wet dream for petrolheads – Jeremy Clarkson's idea of heaven.

On the engineering front the progress from the earliest BMW car (would you believe, based on an Austin Seven) to the latest prototypes of electric cars is a remarkable narrative of technological development, and one which forces you to think about what may happen in the next fifty years as technological development accelerates still further. It poses questions about the nature of the car of the future – its shape, capability, electronics, safety, power source and environmental impact. But the answers may also be affected by possible changes to the way we organise our mobility.

Google and others are experimenting with driverless cars in order to answer some of the technological questions. Mercedes are working on self-driving trucks. At the same time the Uber online booking system is proving a disruptive force in the taxi industry, as we have seen in France. Volunteer car sharing groups are also raising questions about different concepts of ownership. At some point the questions raised by these separate developments are bound to inter-connect, and have unexpected consequences. For instance, the concept of car sharing is forcing insurance companies to think about risk in an entirely different way.

Despite these developments the cathedral-like spaces of BMW Welt betray no sense of vulnerability about a business model that relies on personal ownership of and identification with the car. The theatrical arrangements for the delivery of new cars in this gargantuan space take on the air of religious ritual, a visit to the temple. It may be that the size of developing markets such as China means that the business model has much life in it yet. The car industry's investment in individual consumer aspirations – which BMW Welt is designed to reinforce – is such that only a fool would anticipate the majority falling out of love with the car anytime soon.

But it is the issues of industrial policy, particularly ownership, that confront the British visitor head on. In a large space a few yards from the entrance a Rolls Royce Phantom is a model of gleaming haughtiness. Close by are signs to the BMW museum with its display of the history of the Mini that commands an even bigger space. Both Rolls Royce and the Mini are now owned by BMW. The British visitor (of a certain age) is hit by the poignancy of the juxtaposition of the letters BMW and BMC, synonyms for respective success and failure. In both cases the B stands for geographic identity – British in the case of BMC – the British Motor Corporation – and Bavaria in the case of BMW – Bayerische Motoren Werke. The blue and white quartered badge of the German car represents the Bavarian flag.

Their stories could not have been more different. BMC came to stand for British industrial ineptitude, a toxic mix of managerial complacency and incompetence and union intransigence, memorably sent up by Peter Sellers in the film *I'm all right, Jack*. BMC was not even a brand, but parent to a self-defeating fragmentation between its competing brands – Austin, Morris, Wolseley, MG and Riley – brands that mimicked the British obsession with class. It even imposed this 'brand-engineering' nonsense on the Mini itself – variously, an Austin Seven, Morris Mini-Minor, Riley Elf or Wolseley Hornet – ensuring that despite its technical novelty the Mini lost £20 per car for the company. BMC is no more.

In contrast, BMW has always been a single brand, imposed on both its cars and motorcycles, brilliantly and consistently developed over the long term. BMC was content to sell poorly made cars to protected

Commonwealth markets, BMW sold to Europe and then the world, notably in recent years to China. In 2014 it had revenues of €80.4 billion. (In the same year Mercedes had revenues of just short of €130 billion, and Audi €53 billion.) Ponder these figures when you next read of Britain's ballooning trade deficit or that EU membership is an obstacle to selling globally.

How to respond? Is the gut reaction simply silly injured *amour propre*? After all, you may say that as an ardent European this should not worry me. Isn't the Mini still made in the UK? Isn't the integration of European industry just what the founders of the European project wanted? Isn't that why they started by merging the coal and steel industries? Yes, but it is of concern when the movement is so one-sided. It is not true that ownership does not matter. One simple reason is that in 2014 BMW made a profit of €8.7 billion on its €80.4 billion revenues. That accrues primarily to the country of ownership not the country of manufacture. Ownership can also dictate the location of investment and particularly the location of research and development. The Welsh economy found this out the hard way when the manufacturing plants of vaunted inward investors moved east after the collapse of the Soviet Union.

Last year, when the ONS looked at foreign ownership of British companies, it found that the number of foreign owned companies had actually dropped by three per cent since 2009, but that their total contribution to GVA had increased by nineteen per cent. That was explained by a ten per cent drop in the number of foreign owned micro-businesses employing fewer than ten people. The number of small, medium and large sized foreign owned companies

– who make a much bigger contribution to the economy and to exports – had actually increased. The U.S., Germany and the Netherlands were the three biggest UK company owners. Only a few years ago it was reported that foreign corporations controlled thirty-nine per cent of UK patents far more than foreign owned patents in the US (11.8%) Japan (3.7%) and the EU as a whole (13.7%). Lest anyone jump to the wrong conclusion, this has nothing to do with the EU. Other EU member countries are just better at protecting their own industries.

Ownership also matters in the public utilities. James Meek, in his book *Private Island* has charted the takeover of water, rail and bus companies, sometimes by private equity companies – as in the water industry, though not in Wales![8] – but sometimes, with the deepest irony of all, by public utility companies from other European countries. Scotrail is owned by the Dutch company, Abellio, the international arm of the Dutch national rail operator. The southeastern and London Midland services are owned by Keolis, jointly owned by SNCF, the state-owned French rail company and the Quebec Deposit & Investment Fund. Arriva Trains Wales that operate on the Valleys Line that runs past my Cardiff home is owned by Deutsche Bahn, a private German rail operator that carried me in much greater comfort between Munich and Nuremberg than it did between Cardiff and Welshpool yesterday.

Strange how the erosion of our industrial base has never been a central issue in this country, not in any general election in my lifetime, or even in the current contest for the leadership of the party of labour.

---

[8] Since 2001 Welsh Water has been a not-for-profit business where all profits are re-invested in the company for the benefit of customers.

## 7 March 2016

## Too many campaigns

Like it or not Wales, Scotland and London are going to have to conduct elections to their own democratic bodies on 5 May under the overshadowing umbrella of the referendum on Britain's membership of the European Union on 23 June. In Wales and Scotland the ability of their own governments to carry out their manifestos will be affected by a decision that the whole of Britain will take six weeks later. For that reason, if for no other, we cannot wait until after those elections to begin to remind Welsh electors of just what is at stake. For there is a difference.

Without in any way belittling elections to our National Assembly, the truth is that whatever the outcome there will be another election in 2021. The referendum on Europe, on the other hand, is going to determine the future of the whole of these islands for generations to come. Whatever Michael Howard or Boris Johnson or Nigel Farage may tell you, it is unlikely there will be a second chance in the foreseeable future, not least because a British exit will almost certainly diminish sharply any trust in Britain amongst the other members of the European Union. 'Perfidious Albion' will have lived up to the centuries-old jibe.

Less than four months is not a long time in which to counter decades of anti-EU myth-making and 'little Englander' prejudices that have been thrust down the throats of the British public by a predominantly hostile press. Those papers have echoed political parties and factions that, if truth be told, have always been hostile to British identification with Europe – sometimes from an innate xenophobia, sometimes from a romantic view of Britain's past and an unrealistic view of its present and future, and sometimes from more tawdry personal political calculation. In the short time ahead, the work of bringing home the realities of today's dangerously uncertain world will be a key task for Wales: Stronger in Europe, part and parcel of the Britain: Stronger in Europe campaign. We will also have to remind people of the tangible importance of the EU in our lives. Europe is not 'them', it is 'us'. To mention but a few headlines:

Wales benefits from our membership more than any other part of the UK and is due to receive more than £3bn of EU investment between 2014 and 2020; Welsh farmers will receive £1.7bn between now and 2020 and enjoy branding protection for Welsh beef and lamb; the European Investment Bank has invested £1.6bn in Welsh projects over the past twenty years; Welsh exports to the EU are worth £5.4bn; More than 190,000 jobs in Wales are linked to our European trade; our tourism trade has benefited from investment in developments such as the coastal path, while European water directives have ensured cleaner waters and beaches around our coast.

It is an acknowledged danger of referendums that voters are affected by extraneous issues that are not directly related to the question on the ballot paper. It will be our task to remind the Welsh public of just what is at stake for the Welsh and British economies and employment, for working conditions, for our environment, our consumer and social protection, our national security, Britain's place in the world and, let us not forget, the future of Europe.

Those who would have us disengage from the EU complain that supporters of the EU are indulging in Project Fear. But only the ineffably foolish or the blind can believe that there is nothing to fear in the world today. The clouds are many and some are very dark indeed: the bloody turmoil in the Middle East and in north Africa ripping states apart and creating the greatest movement of peoples since 1945; international terrorism that can hit the streets of any capital; a weakening world economy and the possibility of another global financial collapse; the economic challenges from China; Russia's resumed aggressiveness under Putin, much of it aimed at dividing the EU; the revived authoritarianism of some East European countries, some of them EU member states; an unpredictable nuclear-armed North Korea; the challenge of climate change.

And let's not forget the chilling prospect of Donald Trump's raging ego eyeing the White House. Are we to believe that all these threats are just an illusion, things to be casually waved away, with a Farage grin or a Johnsonian chortle? Are we to believe there are no obstacles at all to the smooth creation of a post-Brexit land of milk and honey? Of course not. Well-run companies and charities constantly update a risk register in order to lessen the risk of being taken unawares by internal and external events. Those of us who wish to remain in the EU have no illusions about the difficulties and dangers that lie ahead, or about the need for the EU – the institution and some policies – to continue to change. But the Brexit camp would seem to have no risk register. Despite arguing for a wholly unprecedented event – the very first withdrawal of a country from the

EU – the 'Leavites' cleave to a view that all will remain for the best in the best of all possible worlds. They will pass by on the other side of all Europe's problems.

No economic or business disruption, no adverse reactions from any member of the European family, swift and trouble free negotiations not only with the EU but with other countries around the world, no impact on our currency or credit, no risks for our financial services, no impact on our security despite the end of European Arrest Warrants, watertight borders – despite the experience of other non-EU countries – and the complete replacement of EU funding for our farmers and poorer regions via a beneficent Treasury. In short, a path of action with not a single downside. Project Fantasy. It's not a world I recognise or can imagine.

The EU has been a blessing for Europe, binding its wounds after three of the bloodiest decades in its history, reviving economies that were on their uppers, giving countries such as Spain, Portugal and Greece a route-map from dictatorship to democracy, ensuring that countries once beyond the Iron Curtain were brought into the democratic fold, securing a powerful place for Europe in a globalised world. It might yet hold Britain together against Scottish pressures. It is true that in recent years, under exceptional external pressures, the EU has not always been surefooted. Some dislike the imposition of an austerity agenda – imposed, it has to be said, at the behest of some key *national* governments. Many of its friends are currently critical, and can sketch a dozen ways in which it might change for the better. But even the most critical do not see the answer in desertion by the largest member of the family outside the Eurozone. For one of the biggest risks arising from Brexit is to the EU itself. Many of those who would have us leave the EU still want it to remain intact and be there to be the single market with which we will negotiate a different future. But what if Brexit were to be an event that destabilises Europe itself? After all, it has internal enemies aplenty in several member states.

My own generation has been blessed by an exceptionally long period of European peace and an unprecedented increase in economic prosperity. In the process a larger proportion of the British population has travelled to and known other parts of Europe than in any previous peacetime generation in history. We should all want that freedom and that sense of common purpose to be there for our children and grandchildren. We can, to borrow a recently used phrase, be better together. But we will have to work for it.

## 12 April 2016

# The Know-Nothing party

There is a thread in current political debate – whether in elections at different levels or in the debate on our membership of the EU – that is sometimes described as a battle of the people versus the establishment. It is not an unusual phenomenon in history, neither in the past has it been restricted to one country. But there are real dangers in exaggerating this supposed divide.

The reflexes of London's tabloid press insist on the dominance of the populist view, often regardless of whether or not such views are actually shared by a majority. If we were to believe that the splenetic headlines of the Daily Mail or the Daily Express on the European issue somehow express 'the popular view', we would be hard pressed to explain why, in most polls, a majority are now in favour of Britain remaining in the EU. The truth is that the majority of people are a little more level-headed than London's tabloid editors, and usually pretty reluctant to align themselves with conviction politicians at the far end of the political spectrum, whether far right or far left.

In this country a healthy balance between scepticism of authority and common sense democratic instincts may get out of kilter from time to time, but the pendulum cannot stay swung far out for long without defying the gravitational pull that the solid centre exerts. It is for this reason that some in UKIP know that real electoral success requires them to curb some of the instincts of the beast they have created. It is their difficulty in doing this that gives the game away. It is a nasty party, as fractious and divisive internally as externally. Many of its dogs are not house-trained, while the dog-owners tend to turn a blind eye to any canine misdemeanour. The pity is that its internal disputes – that seem habitual – tend to get a lot less coverage than divides in more mainstream parties.

UKIP has a strange resemblance to the party that flourished for a short period in the United States in the middle of the 19th century – the Know-Nothings. They were nativist, equivocal on slavery and anti-immigrant – anti-Catholic immigration in the American case – with the Pope in the 19th century caricatured as the source of all evil in much the same way as the European Commission is lampooned by UKIP today. Unlike UKIP, the Know-Nothings achieved some real electoral success – such as control of Massachusetts – although their rise and fall was encompassed in scarcely more than seven years between 1849 and 1856. It is instructive that the two American politicians who were later tagged with the Know-Nothing label were George Wallace, the segregationist governor of Alabama, in the 1960s, and Donald Trump today. UKIP are Britain's Know-Nothings – carrion crows, feeding where they can on poverty and disorientation in this unsettlingly fast-moving, unstable and dangerous world.

This is a party that, at its recent conference in North Wales was selling, or raffling, a copy of German invasion plans from 1940, Dad's Army DVDs, and a tea-cloth libelling Herman Van Rompuy, the president of the EU, in the most racist way. Whatever else transpires in Thursday's poll for the National Assembly, we must all hope that the better instincts of the Welsh people – democratic, compassionate, internationalist – will come to the fore and reject UKIP utterly.[9]

In recent weeks countless people from many parts of the political spectrum have expressed the view to me that the prospect of a UKIP cohort in the National Assembly would be depressing indeed, comprised as it would likely be of a strong carpet-bagging element, and a candidate in South East Wales, whose overt racism has been an embarrassment even to his fellow party members – though not sufficiently embarrassing for them to require him to stand down.

---

[9] They didn't. UKIP won 13% of the votes and seven seats via the regional list system.

It is hard to see what Wales could possibly gain from Neil Hamilton's offer to us of the fag-end of his ropey, not to say seedy career, or from Mark Reckless's sudden discovery that we exist at all. Even their own leader in Wales didn't want them, such is the chaos in the UKIP high command. Is it really at the behest of such 'here today – gone tomorrow' people that we are going to grant them seats on the edge of our national platform in order to distract our democratic Assembly from its core work? And all to facilitate a quite separate task of urging us to take a double leap, forward into the dark and backward into a past – a past which, if it ever existed, cannot be recreated today? Like the Know-Nothings any marginal success for UKIP – if it comes – in Thursday's election will prove short-lived: candidates elected on one day, and the purpose of their existence gone a mere seven weeks later. Best if Wales does not add votes for UKIP to our unwanted waste.

## 20 April 2016

# A lop-sided debate

Only a week into the official campaign period the EU referendum is hitting its lop-sided stride, with the main strands becoming apparent very quickly.

On the Remain side an extraordinary weight of organised opinion has weighed in – the UK Treasury, the Governor of the Bank of England, the CBI, our trade unions, our farming unions, not to mention critical external observers such as the IMF, eight former US

Treasury Secretaries, and now the President of the United States. On the Brexit side, the gap left by the surprising absence of any authoritative economic analysis has been filled by abusive rhetorical bluster from Boris Johnson – who called the Prime Minister the 'Gerald Ratner of British politics' – and a standup comic routine from Michael Gove, who attempted to satirise his opponents and the EU, and then offered us an Albanian option for our future – an option that some might have thought beyond satire.

There is room to argue over figures – there always is – but however much people might want to challenge the precision of the Treasury estimates of the price that Britain would pay for leaving the UK, its forecasts would have to be massively out of kilter to turn a minus into a plus. Against such detailed analysis, rhetoric alone does not put much weight into the scales. So far there is not a single serious economic commentator who has calculated an unequivocal economic plus for Britain if we leave the EU.

Vote Leave has also failed to present a single vision of an alternative future for this country. On the contrary, we have been pointed variously to Norwegian, Swiss and Canadian models, while Boris Johnson even executed a false start to the campaign by suggesting that a vote to leave the EU would result in a further negotiation simply to seek better terms. This idea was ditched rather quickly, since even his own allies did not buy it.

Michael Gove, meanwhile, seemed to pour cold water on all these options, suggesting that we had no interest in the single market, preferring instead a pick 'n' mix approach to negotiating trade terms. This approach would give us at least two problems: first, it would actually deepen the uncertainty facing large swathes of British business. It would also prolong that uncertainty by extending the timetable for reaching a new stability. Which industries would Mr Gove prioritise for this multi-headed negotiation? Who would be at the front of the queue and who would be at the back? On how many fronts would we then have to negotiate?

He seems to be willing to pay this price, if only for the emotional high of saying good-bye to the EU, to have sight of that will o' the wisp, sovereignty, and to have the chance of pocketing the money we currently pay to the EU in dues. On the latter point, I fear the money will have disappeared down a hole of Mr Gove's own making. The belief that all that is needed to conjure a British economic miracle is a wave of Mr Gove's rhetorical wand is, frankly, for the fairies.

Economic performance across the countries of Europe has just as much to do with national policies, even when the EU provides a fair and helpful framework and an internal market of more than five hundred million people. It is not the EU that ordained the collapse of British manufacturing. It is not the EU that sold Cadbury to Kraft. It is not the EU that sold Boots the Chemist to a private equity company. It is not Europe that made our big corporations and our banking system so short termist when compared with their German counterparts. If the creation of sunlit uplands is so easy, why hasn't it been in someone's manifesto – here, in Britain.

Mr Gove also seems to blame the EU for the condition of Spain, Italy and Greece. But the real blame here rests much more with a single country: Germany's obsessive adherence to economic austerity – a policy that Mr

Gove's own government supports. I did not hear our Chancellor suggesting to Mrs Merkel that she cut southern Europe a better deal.

It is not clear to me whether the Brexit brigade want to negotiate a deal with the EU's single market (in which case we will have to pay a budgetary contribution) or to see that single market unravel (in which case the economic prospects of Europe would be black indeed, Britain included). However much the Brexit team twiddle their Rubik's cube, there is one piece that won't fit. When I hear the Remain side being accused of Project Fear, I like to point out that it is not us who dug the empty hole down which we are asked to peer.

There is one *mea culpa* that can be justly required of the British political and business establishment. It is implicit in several questions posed in a *Western Mail* editorial yesterday. It asked why, if the EU is so important, it has been defended so half heartedly by so many in the political establishment, and why it has been presented as a necessary evil rather than proudly championed. There is truth in the charge. The pro-EU side in British politics kept its head down for far too long. Within parties, politicians looked over their shoulders at internal opponents. Too many have been half-hearted members of the club, reluctant to credit, ready to whinge; too ready, also, to see every reasonable agreement or compromise in Europe as either a victory or a defeat. In this it has been abetted by an outrageously partisan press, amongst which the *Western Mail* is a notable exception.

We all need to remind people insistently over the coming weeks of what the EU has done for peace, security and prosperity – for jobs and working conditions, for students and education, for agriculture and the environment. That is a record of no mean achievement. And if you are looking for a Project Hope, then I believe that the EU's imperfections constitute an agenda to which the UK should commit its creative energies and diplomatic talents full-heartedly. That is a change project more exciting, more promising and less vain (in both senses) than Mr Gove's attempt at backward time travel. To remain in the EU is undoubtedly the less risky road, but it is by no means a road short of tough challenges to help ourselves and the whole European family to thrive in a dangerous world.

7 May 2016

## Call to arms

There is a rumour going round that that those who want to see Britain remain a member of the European Union are somehow lacking in passion, while those who would have us leave are full of 'passionate intensity'. It is time to quash the first of these perceptions emphatically.

For the past few months the campaign to Remain In has been complicated by the parallel National Assembly election campaign, where parties have, inevitably, concentrated on fighting each other. Welsh broadcasters, too, faced with conflicting guidelines for elections and referenda, have been keen to keep debate on the European issue out of election coverage. But with those elections out of the way the field is now clear to concentrate on the issue that is going to shape the future of Wales and the UK for generations to come. So important is the issue that I confidently predict there will no lack of obvious passion on the Remain side in the next seven weeks. It will come not only from the official campaign but from many and varied parts of society.

It has been easy over the last forty-three years of EU membership to take Europe for granted. It is, in fact, one measure of the success of our relationship. Europe has been an ever-present dimension of our existence – our work and leisure and culture, the physical environment and the environment of the mind – to the extent that it is now part of our sub-conscious. As people unpack these elements of Europe that they have absorbed so fully, they may realise that it matters, and that leaving the EU would entail fundamental and deeply unwelcome changes to their lives, their society and the national mindset.

Peace and security matters to people, as was evident in the huge scale of the demonstration against British involvement in Iraq, or the massive public demonstrations in Paris after successive terrorism attacks. People know that this is a dangerous world, and that it is already less stable than the peaceful world that Europe managed to build after the last world war – a period of peace unprecedented in four centuries. They can feel that tightening of the gut when Putin flexes his muscles in Georgia or the Ukraine, or when the North Korean President talks of his nuclear weapons as if they were a new toy. They know that a European Union that keeps twenty-eight countries – many of them free of totalitarian rule for less than thirty years – talking together on a daily basis, has to be a better option than the unpredictability of an unstructured free for all.

Europe matters to Welsh businesses that have invested time and effort in building a sound European market for their goods, often accounting for more than half of their total exports. Europe matters to Welsh farmers who look to the EU for more than 90% of their export trade. Europe matters to university researchers that are advancing our knowledge and building the foundations of the economy of the future. Europe matters to all those individual employees and their families whose work life balance has been underpinned by European insistence on good working conditions. Europe's level playing field matters for our material prosperity.

But our relationship with our European partners is much more than a cash transaction. It helps shape an outward looking view of the world. Europe matters to Welsh students who are enriched forever by studying in other European countries or by studying here alongside other European students. Europe matters to authors and film-makers, musicians and artists here in Wales and throughout the EU, who can travel and work without let or hindrance, celebrating our diversity and commonality. I know from my own experience with Welsh National Opera, that we have active relationships with twenty opera houses in eleven different European countries. I also know how enriching that has been for the company and for our audiences. It is a process of deep sharing that is by now second nature.

At the outset of the campaign one of the leaders of Vote Leave, Michael Gove, described the EU as "mired in the past". As so often with Vote Leave, their assertions stand reality on its head: as when attachment to Europe is described as 'parochial', or when an extension of our sovereignty through the EU, is described as sacrificing our sovereignty. As the highly respected commentator, Martin Wolf, wrote in the Financial Times last week, "Treaties do not undermine sovereignty, they express it... They constrain the exercise of sovereignty, with the intention of making it more effective... Membership [of the EU] gives the UK a say in the future of the continent. It gives it a potent voice in the positions on global affairs of one of the world's most powerful actors. It magnifies the UK's ability to influence global developments that are of vital interest to its citizens."

It is Vote Leave that is mired in the past, mired in an Anglo-centric imperial nostalgia that is rejected by Commonwealth leaders in Canada and New Zealand, just as Mr Gove's Albanian model of Britain's trading future has been rejected by the President of Albania. The Vote Leave view of the world is one that pre-dates low cost air travel, the Channel Tunnel, the internet, and global talks on trade and climate change – not to mention two world wars. It is a view of the world and of our future that, on 23 June, will be rejected decisively by a Wales that will show itself once again on the progressive side of history.

13 June 2016

## Gordon Brown – man with a plan

Gordon Brown has done the referendum debate a huge favour by outlining a positive agenda for the EU in the next decade. In doing so he has displayed that characteristic grasp of the big picture that was so evident in his decisive contribution to tackling the financial crisis back in 2008 – a contribution for which he has not yet been given the credit he deserves. He has also reminded us that the UK has a golden opportunity to launch this agenda next year when it is our turn to occupy the Presidency of the EU. This is the best possible riposte to Brexiters who would have us withdraw from a position of influence in Europe and the world, and actually increase the vulnerability of those at the bottom of the economic pile. It may have been intended as a particular message for Labour supporters, but its significance is much wider than that.

He has got away from forecasts that are often discounted by the public even when they have validity, to concentrate instead on a programme of action that takes account of the real and inescapable dynamic of this interconnected world. This is the kind of agenda that can begin to rekindle the idealism on which the EU was founded in the aftermath of war. It involves applying the principles of the single market to the digital economy, the energy market and the service sector, in ways that could not only kick-start a real revival in the European economy, but also create more jobs and bring real benefits to the lives of people who have suffered some of the negative impacts of globalisation. This is an agenda that has a supreme relevance for Wales, whether in the creation of more jobs in the digital economy, the use of the EU's €315bn infrastructure fund for communities hit by industrial change, or protecting the rights of the most vulnerable workers.

The Brexit campaign has tried to dismiss the current £245m a year net benefit that Wales receives from the

EU, by saying that these strands of EU funding will end in 2020. This has always seemed a silly argument, for two reasons: first, the programmes that benefit Wales are fundamental to the purposes of the EU and will continue in some form beyond 2020; second, if the more extreme Brexiters had their cavalier way the funding would stop much earlier.

Gordon Brown's agenda reflects the EU's long-standing commitment to regional development and hints at the possible direction and scale of funding well beyond 2020. It is also a balanced agenda that embraces the economic and social dimensions, whereas all that Brexiters offer is a tsunami of deregulation that would not be in the interests of consumers or of hard-pressed working people. In a world where middle order jobs seems to have disappeared, why would we listen to Brexit's right wing economists – those on Planet Minford[10] – who say we shouldn't worry if leaving the EU leads to "the elimination of manufacturing". Tell that to the 151,000 people in manufacturing in Wales – in Airbus and Toyota in north Wales, or to steelworkers in Port Talbot and Llanwern, or to Ford workers in Bridgend.

Gordon Brown has reminded us that those who would have us leave the EU want the UK to be out of step with the world. In an era when big business is multi-national, when research has become increasingly collaborative and international, when climate change knows no boundaries, when tax avoiders leap over lines on the map, the Leavers would have us demolish the forty-three-year-old bridge

---

[10] Professor Patrick Minford, Cardiff Business School and leading light in 'Economists for Brexit' during the referendum campaign.

we have to the biggest single integrated market in the world. They would have us withdraw from a close international partnership to live on the fringes of everywhere.

Too much is made of the fact that the UK is an island. In the age of cheap air travel and the internet, not to mention our Channel Tunnel, no country is an island. But even the people of this island must know that a Europe-wide energy pool makes sense. You cannot tackle tax avoidance and the problem of tax havens in one country alone. Gordon Brown is absolutely right to say that we need "the collective clout a united Europe can bring to bear".

And on the vexed question of immigration – that derives not from the sins of the EU, but from the phenomenon of the biggest mass movement of peoples as the result of war since 1945 – Brown also offers a practical response. Not the self-defeating erection of barriers that would bring our public services to a halt, but the creation by the EU of a much bigger fund – "an enhanced solidarity fund" – to help communities where migration trends have put undue pressure on hospitals, schools and other services.

In short, Gordon Brown has injected a welcome note of promise. It is by no means an exhaustive agenda for the development and reform of the EU. But in a period when many countries, including the UK, are seeing the consequences of alienation from politics and disaffection with rampant inequality, the overdue message is that we are not powerless. There are things that governments can do, but only when we act together – especially with the neighbours with whom we share this continent.

22 June 2016

## Fantasies and facts

Tomorrow we will be able to cast our votes on the biggest question we have faced in almost half a century, perhaps bigger than any we may face in our lifetime. It will shape our lives and our country for the foreseeable future. It may even change the politics of a continent. It will also say a lot about who we are.

Passions have been stoked by the fact that it is a clear binary choice – weighty and possibly irreversible – by the closeness of the polls, and a long-standing cynicism about politics in general and about the EU in particular. But nothing can excuse Nigel Farage's repugnant poster, nor Vote Leave's unrelenting promotion of an acknowledged lie about our financial contribution to the EU. It is in keeping only with the merciless misrepresentation and perpetuation of myths that the EU has endured for decades in Britain. Large parts of the press have given it credit for nothing and the blame for most things.

This has obscured from view any list of the tangible benefits that the European venture has brought to the whole continent, benefits that Vote Leave would have us throw away for a wholly illusory risk-free future that would start to crumble in their hands on Friday morning as the world's markets recoiled. There cannot be an infallible guide to the future, only probabilities. And the whole world – whether they are heads of state in North America, Europe or the old Commonwealth, economists or manufacturers or environmentalists – is telling us,

Don't jump. It makes no sense to put our fingers in our ears at the sound of that massed chorus.

Voters often say they want facts. They deserve a factual understanding of the real impact of the EU on their own lives. It is a fact that the European single market, with its 510 million consumers, is bigger than the USA. Europe's GDP is $1 trillion greater than America's GDP. It is a fact that we are the second largest country in that union, with all the clout that goes with that, and that it is our biggest single market. It is also a fact that our membership of the EU does not in any way prevent us from trading with the rest of the world.

It is a fact that the EU has been crucial in making the UK and Wales highly successful in winning foreign investment, with no less than five hundred companies in Wales alone owned by companies from other EU states. It is a fact that 190,000 Welsh jobs are linked to our trade with the EU, and that Wales gets back £245m a year more than it contributes – universities benefiting from hefty research income, and farmers receiving about 80% of their income *from* the EU and sending all but a tiny fraction of their exports *to* the EU.

It is a fact that the EU has been a guarantor of better conditions for the employed as well as the disabled, and of a multitude of safeguards for consumers. It is a fact that more people now travel more often to other European countries than ever before in our history – a direct result of the EU Open Skies policy that broke up monopolies and allowed the emergence of budget airlines. We would not be making cheaper calls from our mobiles across Europe, were it not for EU action to end roaming charges. It is a fact that our rivers and beaches have never been cleaner. We would not be taking pride in Wales's profusion of Blue Flag beaches had it not been for the EU's water framework directive. We should not forget that as late as the early 1990s most of our sewage was going out to sea untreated.

But in this dangerous, volatile world we must value the EU for more than a list of localised benefits. The most important fact of all is that Western Europe has enjoyed the longest period of peace in many centuries, and the greatest increase in the general standard of living in history. It is also a fact that the EU has also helped democratise Europe. In 1936 two hundred Welshmen, mainly from the mining valleys, went to fight against Franco's fascists in Spain. They did not succeed. Forty-one years later the European Community's tough but canny approach helped ensure the democratisation of Spain. Its entry to the European Community followed in the 1980s along with that of Greece and Portugal, two other countries shepherded out of dictatorship. It is a fact that after the collapse of the Iron Curtain in 1989 the existence of the EU ensured that the countries of Eastern Europe were drawn into the democratic fold – although there is still work to be done in some countries to embed the full range of democratic norms. It is a fact that the EU provided an essential element for the peace deal in Northern Ireland, still a vitally important element today.

Even aware of these facts, we also have to assess judgments about the future, to assess the probabilities. If you are still undecided I would find a quiet corner and ask yourself five common sense questions: i) Is being inside a market of 510 million people likely to be better for our economy than being outside it? ii) Do I know of many clubs where non-members get exactly the same benefits as members? iii) Are there aspects of my agreed working conditions – paid holidays, maternity leave, redundancy guarantees – that I would be happy to give up? iv) Am I confident that a UK government pledged to reduce borrowing will replace every penny of EU income that currently comes to Wales's communities, businesses, farmers, universities and training centres? v) In this dangerous world do we need more international collaboration or less, more understanding or less, more compassion or less?

Voting to Remain will not solve every problem but neither will it add to them unnecessarily as Vote Leave would have us do. There will still be work to do – but with our neighbours. In the polling booth we must hope, as Abraham Lincoln did in an even darker moment, that we will be 'touched by the better angels of our nature'.

# REFERENDUM AFTERMATH

## 3 July 2016

## A disfiguring event

Last Friday, 1st July 2016, was, as we all know, the 100th anniversary of the start of the Somme offensive in which by its end more than a million men from the European nations and the British Commonwealth were killed or injured. That evening at the Royal Opera House Welsh National Opera performed its newly commissioned opera, *In Parenthesis*, based on the experiences of the poet David Jones at one of the Somme's constituent battles, Mametz Wood. For many of us the power and poignancy of the opera only intensified the unbearable irony of the juxtaposition of this anniversary with the result of the referendum on our membership of the European Union.

For almost half the nation it had already been a week of mourning. Those who had gone to bed at the end of voting day, reassured by Nigel Farage's premature conceding of defeat, awoke to the knowledge that their world had changed. Yes, it was like a sudden bereavement. That terrible empty feeling of incomprehension. An inability to focus on anything else. A pathetic wish to rerun time's tape so that this time the crash would not happen. A questioning of things done and not done, a scramble to pinpoint anything that might have diverted us all from what actually did happen. Then as one grey mist cleared, a red mist descended – a growing anger at fate's multi-headed conspiracy.

There are millions of people who will have shared that experience in the days since 23 June – people who have never believed that Europe starts at Calais, people for whom their citizenship of Europe – passport and all – was a source of pride or, alternatively, who may have taken it for granted, part of the natural order of things. They have all felt this harsh jolt. Others will have felt an even more piercing hurt: citizens of other member states who have made their own lives – and marriages – here; men and women who are and have thought themselves deeply embedded in their adopted communities, sharing in their problems, making their own distinct contribution, so that any sense of difference had, until now, been rendered immaterial except in the sense of enriching our sensibilities with their own. Theirs is a different, sharper pain.

After such a disfiguring event for the country the natural response would be look to a healing process, except that the immediate logic of the result is to make the rupture permanent. To sever ourselves from this union of forty-three years standing will, in a formal sense, lock in a reduced joint responsibility for each other across this continent. It will not be reduced to zero – many will do what they can to maintain networks of interest – but that will not be the same as whole nations operating together, day after day, year after year, the standing mechanisms of collaboration. The means to reach out will be, at the very least, much diminished.

All this would be hard enough to bear had it resulted from some *force majeure* – a natural calamity or a physical sundering of the ground, an inundation such as that which created the English Channel aeons ago. What makes it unbearable is the knowledge that it has been the result of a few months of ugly campaigning in which the Remain side's realism – although often too stridently expressed – was not tempered with enough hope or idealism, and in which the Leave side indulged in a stubborn and unbridled mendacity such as we have not seen in our lifetime – a procession of lies. The latter were aided by UKIP's strut in the deepest gutter of debate – a thinly disguised thuggery of the word that, no matter how indirectly, was echoed in the frenzied murder of a young idealistic woman, Jo Cox, who had dedicated her life to her neighbour and her neighbour's neighbour wherever they might be found in the world. Her life was and is a standing reproof to UKIP's ugliness and what it has unleashed in too many mouths.

It is not only with hindsight that one can see the obstacles to a Remain victory: the aftermath of the 2008 financial collapse; the unremitting, decades-long denigration of European institutions by large sections of the press; world-wide public alienation from political processes; the knowledge that the Conservative party has long been riven on the issue; the emergence of the first Labour leader in decades with no enthusiasm for the European project; and the eclipse of the most pro-EU party, the Liberal Democrats, in the 2015 election.

Against those underlying conditions, the package that David Cameron brought back from his rather desperate negotiation never looked convincing whatever the value of each constituent part. That is why, whatever the shortcomings of the Remain campaign, one has to look beyond it for some explanation of the result. If, as I believe, this was a cry of rage by the 'left behind', in Wales one can look back to the decimation of the Welsh economy during the Thatcher years, or the inevitable downside of single party rule at the local level for half a century and more. But for the moment let's stick to the last decade.

A singular feature of the referendum campaign was the almost total absence of references to the financial collapse of 2007-8. Perhaps the most surprising thing about the decade that followed has been the relative lack of overt public anger. I stress 'overt' because it beggars belief that the public at large have not resented the way in which they have had to sacrifice their incomes and their own and their children's life chances in order to bail out a banking system that had become a casino, and which managed to escape the imposition of any penalties on its boards and managers or even radical reform. When and where would this resentment surface, as it surely had to?

It did not do so in the elections of 2010 or 2015, except in a perverse, masochistic submission to a tendentious narrative that pinned all the blame on Labour mismanagement, not once but twice. Since Labour colluded by offering no counter – captured in Ed Miliband's ineffective response to a mauling by an election studio audience in 2015 – the party proved an unsatisfactory whipping boy. The 2010 and 2015 results, far from being a catharsis, simply increased the pain via George Osborne's austerity budgets, while the system, the source of all the pain, remained in place with all its inequities.

Arguably, the burgeoning UKIP vote in 2015 and the election of Jeremy Corbyn were two manifestations of post-2008 public frustration, but again both were unsatisfactory. The UKIP vote ended with the election of but one MP, while the vote for Corbyn, although a cry for a more radical response to 2008, was stymied by the fact that Corbyn himself was not obviously suited to government. In this situation it is not surprising that when it came to the EU referendum slightly more than half the country saw its chance to vote for direct action, whatever the consequences. The EU had always been a cat available to be kicked, but now it was placed conveniently close to the public's hobnail boot by David Cameron. The RSPCA should report him to the police.

Nevertheless, the closeness of the result must drive anyone to the conclusion that the referendum was winnable for the Remain side, and especially so here in Wales. After all, the Remain argument had the full and active support of the UK Government, while at times it seemed the whole world was publicly urging us not to jump. In the end it would have required only 41,113 Welsh voters (2.5%) to have changed sides. Across the UK as a whole it would have required only 1.9%, or 634,751, to have done so.

We faced the added – and wholly avoidable – problem of the clash with elections to the National Assembly and Scottish Parliament – either an example of Cameronian carelessness or evidence of a continued inability to see beyond Hadrian's Wall or Offa's Dyke. This certainly delayed and weakened the engagement of party activists in Wales after 5th May. We also faced the major complication of Tata's threat to withdraw from the steel industry in the UK. The First Minster's need to travel to India to meet with Tata scotched plans for an early cross-party launch in the weeks after the Assembly elections.

It says something for the unshakeable nature of current public disillusion that Neath Port Talbot voted Leave, despite the active involvement in the Tata issue of the Welsh Government and one of the area's MPs, Stephen Kinnock, the support of all the steel unions for Remain, and targeted Save our Steel leafletting by Stronger In throughout the locality. It was a not dissimilar story in northeast Wales where Flintshire voted Leave despite Airbus – an employer of six thousand people in the constituency – being one of the most vocal supporters of Remain.

Another setback was the emasculation of civil society by the UK Government's illiberal anti-lobbying regulations and fierce Charity Commission guidelines. In the 2011 referendum in Wales, many civil society organisations became fully engaged in the debates on the proposed new powers for the National Assembly. Many had produced evidence for the All Wales Convention in 2007. By contrast, in this referendum civil society organisations were almost invisible, scared off by the Charity Commission and often by independent legal advice. There may have been ways around the guidelines, but a climate of nervous fear prevailed.

Some have taken the vote to indicate the end of any Welsh distinctiveness in politics. That would be a premature conclusion. If Welsh voters can distinguish between Assembly elections and General Elections, as they do, there is no reason why they should not be able to spot the difference in a referendum on Europe. When one looks at Wales in comparison with the regions of England that voted Leave, we registered the second lowest Leave vote (52.5%), just behind the South East of England (51.8%). One might have expected Wales to register a similar vote to the North East of England, a region that has suffered much the same kind of economic pain – yet the Leave vote there was the third highest – 58% – just behind the West and East Midlands (59.2 and 58.8 respectively).

The vote also created a pecking order of pro-Remain capitals including Edinburgh (74.4), Glasgow (66.6), Bristol (61.7), Manchester (60.4), Cardiff (60), London (59.9), Liverpool (58.2), Newcastle (50.7), and Leeds (50.3). Three cities in the Core Cities Network voted Leave: with Remain scores of – Birmingham (49.6), Nottingham (49.2), and Sheffield (49). It is noteworthy that Cardiff voted marginally more heavily for Remain than London, and ten per cent more than Sheffield, Nottingham, Birmingham, Leeds, and Newcastle. Arguably, political devolution makes a difference.

But such analysis in the context of a referendum may be beside the point. The UK as a whole has taken a decision. How should those who disagree react? The first thing to stress is that it is neither dishonourable nor undemocratic to seek to overturn this result. It is what all defeated parties do after each election. The result was not overwhelmingly in favour of Brexit. It was not a vote in favour of a coherent alternative, or any plan at all. It was achieved on the back of claims that, in another context, would not have got past the Advertising Standards Authority. The time needed to negotiate new arrangements is more than sufficient to allow for a change in public opinion. There is already evidence of buyer's remorse, especially here in Wales. There may even be enough time to see a significant change in attitudes to institutional reform within the EU itself. That said, any reversal of the referendum decision has, in the end, to be by similar democratic means.

In this situation it is in the interests of the UK and of Wales that we do not rush our fences. At the UK level there is a new government to be established, an opposition to be re-shaped, a negotiating team to recruited, and a set of objectives to be formulated, jointly between the UK Government and the devolved administrations. But on the other side, if enough countries within the EU really want to see the United Kingdom remain inside the fold, they will have to work quickly not only to decide on their approach to the coming negotiation, but also to shape an agenda for the EU's own internal reform. In the meantime it is in both our short-term and long-term interests that we should do everything possible to maintain our European networks at every level, and here at home to ensure that, while still citizens of Europe, we continue to make Europe's case.


27 July 2017

## Sport and culture double whammy

The Welsh Government's decision not to pursue a bid for the 2026 Commonwealth Games is going to lead to prolonged recrimination. My guess is that, rightly or wrongly, it will be seen by many as emblematic of a lack of ambition and resolve. That may be unfair, but even unfair judgments have a habit of hanging around for a very long time if people believe they chime with an existing perception. Is there a deeper problem here than this one decision on a specific project?

No-one doubts that governments at all levels in the UK are under financial pressure, and there is no escaping the fact that Brexit has introduced a new element of uncertainty. But on the face of it, there does seem to be a perplexing gap between the cost estimates for the 2026 event for Wales, and the actual costs and benefits for the Glasgow Games in 2014. Since the full feasibility study is not in the public domain, it is not easy to come to a definitive judgment. Anyone familiar with these bidding competitions will know that figures are elastic, with the outturn often depending on what is loaded into the bid and what is kept outside to be deemed normal expenditure. But questions do pile up.

When one looks at comparisons between the Glasgow event and the top line figures for the proposed event in Wales, the obvious question is, are we comparing like for like? If, as the Welsh Minister, Ken Skates, suggested, there are gaps in our sports facilities provision that we need to fill anyway, was too much loaded onto the costs of the Games event rather than deeming some to be an otherwise necessary investment in a continuing facility?

Public funding at Glasgow was split between the city and the Scottish Government, with the city shouldering 20% of the cost. In Wales there has been no commitment by local authorities. Are we now to assume that even the largest Welsh local authorities are no longer able to invest in major international events? Aren't city regions being created to generate this larger capacity? Was any attempt made to pare down the cost figures when they emerged during the study? Is the insistence on an all-Wales bid – which it claimed would have added an extraordinary £220m to the cost – self-defeating. Has the best been the enemy of the good?

Brexit notwithstanding, it is an irony that in the year when Wales's sporting profile has been higher than ever – courtesy of our football team – we cannot steel ourselves for a bold decision to support an international sporting event to be held a decade away. There is a lot here for the Assembly's Health, Social Care and Sport Committee to look at.

One of the things lost in the process has been the obligatory year-long cultural programme that would have led up to the Games. Had the result of the referendum on Europe gone the other way, we might have consoled ourselves with a bid for the European Capital of Culture in 2023. But it appears that, too, has gone away. For the situation is that some of the English and Scottish cities who had declared an interest in bidding for the culture title – Bristol, Leeds, Milton Keynes and Dundee – are intent on continuing to pursue their bids – in Bristol's case after an encouraging meeting with one of the Vice Presidents of the European Commission. It is also worth remembering that the title has occasionally gone to cities outside the EU – Bergen in Norway and Reykjavik in Iceland in 2000 and Istanbul in Turkey in 2010. The EU needs its outreach – which is why the EU's MEDIA programme supports 1,037 cinemas in the Europa Cinemas network in 619 cities and 41 countries across the world.

A bid for Capital of Culture in 2023 would have provided an ideal way to cement together the emerging South East Wales city region, putting socially valuable cultural muscle onto the skeleton of the proposed Metro rail system. Such is the spread of cultural facilities throughout the rest of Wales, together with the touring capacities of our arts organisations, it would have been easy to graft on an all-Wales dimension. Of course, there would be some who would see the seeking of a European title as an affront to the majority in Wales who voted to leave the EU. But, as even our Foreign Secretary, Boris the arch-Leaver, constantly reminds us, we are 'leaving the EU not leaving Europe'. We remain part and parcel of a European civilisation. In that context maintaining access to the EU's cultural programmes and networks must be written into our negotiating objectives for our relationship with the rest of the union.

This double whammy for sport and culture reminds us that the Welsh Government currently lacks a coherent and robust international strategy, one that all interest groups – including sport and culture – understand, support and pursue, and that speaks to our values and our place in the world. If we are pulling out of the EU, we need one in short order.

4 August 2016

## The nasty party

What is it about UKIP? Whether in Wales or across the UK, conspiracy and insult are the order of the day. How can any British political party have so quickly surpassed the Labour Party – and by a country mile – in its addiction to internal warfare? The party of brotherly love, it ain't. A year ago the party's only MP, Douglas Carswell, was calling for the resignation of his leader, the velvet collared Nigel Farage. There was talk of blazing rows between the two men. Meanwhile in a newspaper interview the party's campaign manager described Mr Farage as a "snarling, thin skinned, aggressive man".

Things have scarcely been any better in Wales. Three months ago UKIP's rather rum Welsh cohort was delighting in the election of seven of them to the National Assembly. Within days Nathan Gill, the leader who had delivered this success, had been ousted by his own group, in favour of Mr Neil Hamilton, who is rummer than most. The UKIP Assembly Group, with remarkable persistence – and, let it be said, some justice – is now insisting Mr Gill give up the other seat that he already occupies in the European Parliament.[11] Mr Hamilton is, of course, not on speaking terms with Mr Farage. So Mr Carswell falls out with Mr Farage, who falls out with Mr Hamilton, who falls out with Mr Gill, who never wanted Mr Hamilton in the Assembly in the first place.

By the way, in case you hadn't noticed, Mr Gill was also to be the running mate of leadership candidate, Mr Steven Woolfe, who managed not to submit his application for the leadership ballot in time, to the delight of all but three of the party's national executive committee, a collective that Mr Farage has described as "amongst the lowest grade of people that I have ever met". This is all beyond satire, but

---

[11] Nathan Gill did not resign from the Assembly until December 2017. He is still an MEP.

at least it allows one to ask whether, less than six weeks after the EU referendum, the party has shot its bolt. In a one issue party things are more likely to be, very obviously, very personal. In the Labour Party, fraternal strife is at least dressed up as a matter of policy or competence, although this assumption may not hold good if Mr Corbyn is confirmed in his post.

Nigel Farage can take some of the credit for transforming a widespread disaffection with current politics into a successful anti-EU crusade, but the truth is that the majority of people in this country are usually pretty reluctant to align themselves with the extremes of the political spectrum, whether far right or far left – as even Jeremy Corbyn may eventually realise, even if too late. The recent referendum has sometimes been construed as the people versus the establishment. At times it did seem as if knowledge was a disqualification from the right to hold a view. In this country there has always been a healthy balance between scepticism of authority and common sense democratic instincts. The pendulum will swing from time to time, but it cannot stay swung far out for long without defying the gravitational pull that the solid centre exerts.

If it is not to snatch defeat very quickly from the jaws of victory, and achieve a wider electoral success, UKIP will need to curb some of the instincts of the beast it has created. And I do not include in that description the thousands who have voted for the party, either in elections or in the referendum. They are better people than the party's generals, or corporals. Its leadership can hardly be described as a high command.

29 August 2016

# Resistance is not undemocratic

According to Andrew R T Davies, the Welsh Tory leader, the result of the EU referendum has thrown the Welsh political establishment into a tailspin. It being August, he was not above giving the top an added whipping. Somehow he has managed to command the headlines for twenty-four hours on the subject of the vulnerability of our National Assembly – about which no-one has raised serious concerns – rather than on the more pressing matter of our future relationship with Europe, which concerns us all but about which he had and has no plan to offer.

Let us first of all concede his perfectly fair points that in the Europe referendum the establishment was given a kicking, and that there is a deep sense of antagonism towards the political class. Let us further concede that the Welsh Government may not always have made the best use of the tools available to it, while acknowledging – which Mr Davies did not – that UK Governments have not gone out of their way to help. But then Mr Davies makes an unwarranted leap from our membership of Europe to imply a threat to the legitimacy of our National Assembly, forgetting a number of facts along the way.

One of the ways in which the EU was vulnerable in our referendum was in its perceived lack of democracy. I say perceived, because decisions in the EU are currently taken by elected heads of state and by an elected European Parliament. But critics have had a fair point when they say that even these arrangements have not managed to create any sense of a European *demos*. However, they usually fail to mention the assiduous way in which our media have deliberately and often viciously obstructed such a process. No-one surely would question that there is a sense of a Welsh *demos,* fractious and uncertain though it might be. However hesitant, it was there before the creation of the National Assembly, and post-1999 it allowed the institution to insert itself into the narrative of Welsh life more successfully than sceptics thought possible. One would not deny that there is a British *demos*, despite the differing results in our four nations in the recent referendum or the fact that the UK as a whole was split virtually down the middle.

All recent polling suggests that Welsh people see the National Assembly as having a greater impact on their lives, even than Westminster. It is for that reason that the thrust of constitutional proposals is to entrench its existence – along with that of the Scottish Parliament – in the constitution of the United Kingdom. Ten times more people are calling for it to be given greater powers, than are calling for its abolition.

It is not clear quite what Mr Davies is trying to tell us. Maybe, simply that it would be wise not to take the electorate for granted. Who could quarrel with that? I note that as a claimed 'passionate but pragmatic advocate' of devolution, he is not calling for a referendum on its existence. To be fair to him he has been a more enthusiastic – opponents would say disingenuous – supporter of the devolution of serious taxes than the Welsh Labour administration. Given this apparent concern for the quality of democracy, should one also now look forward to his support for enlargement of the National Assembly, the introduction of electoral reform at all levels of government, open primaries and the extension of the franchise to sixteen and seventeen-year-olds? Rightly or wrongly, these issues are not sitting on the very top of the in-tray in Downing Street or Cardiff Bay. Europe dominates.

Mr Davies' strictures about the National Assembly are in fact a prelude to his main charge that the Welsh Government is "seeking to subvert the result of the referendum", and that "willing Brexit to fail would be disastrous for Wales and disastrous for devolution". He does not mention the disillusion that could occur when the promises of the Brexit proponents prove illusory. It would be easier to deal with his charge if we all knew what Brexit meant. Even Mrs May's Government is struggling to define it, the Chancellor of the Exchequer apparently at odds with his more rabid colleagues. Given this level of uncertainty and imprecision we cannot allow the result of the referendum to stifle all debate or, necessarily, to stand for all time. Writing in the magazine *Prospect*, the economist Anatole Kaletsky argues that the dogma that referendums are sacrosanct is a travesty of true democracy. Democracy requires us, instead, to uphold the principle of continuous challenge. He reminds us that referendums have often been used by dictators to mock democracy on the basis of "One man, one vote, one time". It is for this reason that Germany's post-war constitution excluded the use of referendums. The great champion of representative democracy, Edmund Burke, has, no doubt, been spinning in his grave for some months past.

At the same time we do not yet know what stance other EU countries – still our partners – will take towards the UK, or even how the EU itself will change over the next few years. Concerns about migration effects are widespread in the EU and the UK was never the only country with little appetite for a fully federalist interpretation of 'ever closer union'. With elections in Germany and France and a referendum in Italy all pending in the next twelve months, we do not even know who we will be dealing with. We are surrounded by moving targets, and are one ourselves.

In this unpredictable situation why would any sensible person rule out any particular outcome, within, outside or arm in arm with the EU? What matters is how we define our interests, remembering that they should not be defined solely by a list of projects or by handouts from the public purse, British or European, important though they may be. Welsh politicians, too, will need to take an informed view of a wider British interest. As Nicola Sturgeon reminded Scottish voters a month after the referendum, the interests of any one part of the UK – and of the whole – involves an economic interest, an interest in social protection for our people, in solidarity with other countries – to deal with national security, terrorism, crime and climate change – and in maximising our continuing influence. Protecting all those interests is going to call for open minds.

9 November 2016

# The world just got darker

Oh, God!! I feel terrible. And it's not just the lack of sleep. Did it really happen? And for the second time in less than five months? To wake and know that the world has changed, again. Outside this cottage, three miles from anywhere, on the edge of Snowdonia, lashing rain is drenching the darkness, the stands of oak on this hillside really are rattling in the wind, just as the bard said they did at the death of Llywelyn Fawr – *Poni welwch chwi hynt y gwynt a'r glaw / Poni welwch chwi'r deri'n ymdaraw"*.[12]

Scarcely a day has gone by in the last months when one has not been left open-mouthed at the behaviour of Donald Trump. Nothing has been left unused in his lexicon of offensiveness, no minority left unbelittled, no woman unscorned, no depths unplumbed. Yet no contravention of any one of the norms of decency dented his support. Is this really the champion of the 'left behind'? Is this owner of a towering, gold-plated Manhattan palace, really the Robin Hood of the huddled masses? Or have the put-upon of a transatlantic Sherwood Forest voted for the Sheriff of Nottingham?

Hard to know which was scarier, his campaign speeches or his blithe volte face in his victory address with his talk of "binding the wounds of division", also praising Hillary Clinton's service to the nation, as if he had no culpability for taking a chainsaw to both his opponent and his nation. His attempted expunging of every uttered calumny is breathtaking in its cynicism, underlining a cold contempt for the electorate and his obvious belief that the end justifies the means.

It is understandable that politicians campaign in poetry and govern in prose, but what if you have campaigned with poison? Whether it is winning a presidential election

---

[12] See you not the rush of wind and rain? / See you not the oaks lash each other? – from the medieval Lament for Llywelyn ap Gruffudd, better known as Llywelyn the Great.

or winning a referendum on Britain's membership of the European Union, surely how you win is important. It will not be right to dismiss the content of Trump's campaign as merely the natural excesses of a partisan contest, any more than British people should now ignore the falsehoods on which the Brexit case was made.

The parallels between these two events are legion; indeed, they are part of the same phenomenon. The similarities are being reiterated endlessly on television: a howl of rage of the left behind, an anti-establishment roar, a protest against immigration or globalisation or rampant inequality, or all three, the difference of view between the young and the old and between the most educated and the less educated. There is, too, the stark arithmetic of division in both countries: when set against Hillary Clinton's edging of the popular vote – 47.7% against 47.5% – Britain's 52-48 split in the referendum seems decisive in comparison.

Most difficult of all, in both cases, will be delivering on the expectations raised among the supporters of the victors. No-one can doubt the depth of anger at the negative effects of globalisation and technology on the developed world – the off-shoring of employment, the shrinking of basic industries, the destruction of middle order jobs – but conversely, this has also raised millions in the developing world out of poverty. Yet continuing global imbalances – exacerbated by war, famine and corruption – are still driving some of the biggest migrations of people in centuries. While there is no doubt that the effects of these trends on the home populations of the developed world have to be addressed by politicians, it is the cruellest deception to tell people – whether the poorest or the hard-pressed middle classes – that all can be put right by vapid slogans in television adverts or, even worse, by straight lies on painted battlebuses.

Both Donald Trump and Theresa May are going to be struggling with their economic Rubik's cubes. Mr Trump has promised tax cuts for individuals and businesses that will cost trillions in lost government revenues, and yet has promised to spend $600billion on infrastructure and to sharply increase defence spending, at the same time as taking a protectionist approach to free trade, especially directed against the Chinese whose surpluses are both the mirror image of America's deficits and to a considerable extent the latter's guarantor. It is not even clear that Trump's economics will gain the approval of Republican fiscal disciplinarians in Congress. They certainly will not allow him to become a modern Franklin Roosevelt. Meanwhile, the production of Apple iPhones is not going to be switched from China to America any time soon.

Mrs May meanwhile is still struggling to get her disparate Cabinet members to even agree on a balance of objectives, the Leave campaign having promised simultaneously to deliver tariff free access to Europe, the end of freedom of movement and a reduction in immigration, increased expenditure on the NHS, and no reduction in tax revenues from financial services on which the government has relied for too long. If she comforts herself that swapping Obama for Trump will put Britain further up the queue for a free trade deal with America, just wait until she is faced with a protectionist American president intent on putting America first. He will be content to ride as roughshod over her as he has done over the Scottish countryside. In relation to

America, Britain has surely learnt by now that it is the supplicant, and talk of the special relationship a dollar-free piety to be wheeled out when it suits.

This is not to dismiss the real pain implicit in populist revolt. It has to be addressed, whether in America or Britain or, as we are likely to be reminded in the coming months, in the Netherlands, France and Germany. But it demands an international approach and that the nomadic corporate sector should carry a fair share of the burden. It also demands some change in Germany's fiscal intransigence.

Sadly, this does not exhaust the range of fears furrowing the brow of the international community. The Paris agreement on climate change and the deal with Iran are two other beacons of hope that will suffer if Donald Trump is true to his word. The prospect of mutual admiration between two of the world's most powerful narcissists casts another dark cloud, not least over Eastern Europe – part of a continent for which we still carry responsibility notwithstanding the vote on 23 June. Arguably, in the 1930s the world paid a heavy price for isolationism in America and for unrestrained populism in Germany. What price are we now going to pay for populism in America and a British isolationism within Europe?

26 November 2016

## Peering through the gloom

Scarcely a week goes by at the moment without another conference on the possible consequences of Britain's impending departure from the EU. The latest was held at

Swansea University's new Bay Campus, built with several skips of money from the EU and the European Investment Bank that, even so, were not enough to prevent the city as a whole from voting narrowly to Leave last June. Such conferences can seem repetitive, but they are essential to grow civil society's understanding of the hidden complexities that lay ahead.

The Swansea conference was notable for four things: a contribution from the Welsh Finance Minister, Mark Drakeford, that was a clearer statement on priorities than anything we have yet heard from the UK Government; an impassioned account of the dangers that lie ahead, from Hywel Ceri Jones, a former head of economic and social policy at the European Commission and creator of the Erasmus scheme; an underlining of the legal obstacles the Brexit process has yet to surmount from a professor of international law; and continued evidence of the tactical dilemma that Remainers face in opposing the still imprecise Brexit agenda.

Mark Drakeford outlined ten priorities for the Welsh Government, half of which would have come as no surprise: full and unfettered access to the single market; preservation of as much free movement of people as possible to safeguard its value to such things as the NHS and higher education; confirmation of the permanent status of EU nationals already resident here; guaranteed continuation of the current level of EU funding to Wales; and full maintenance of current social and environmental protections. These five aims are clearly designed to define as soft a Brexit as possible, leading inexorably to a sixth priority which is for a new focus on transitional arrangements – as close as possible to the status quo – to avoid any cliff edge, particularly for business, while longer term agreements are put in place. The remaining four priorities have to do with process, powers and with our future approach to Europe. The first of the quartet is a demand not only for the full involvement of the Welsh Government and the other devolved administrations in shaping the UK Government's view, but also for direct participation by the devolved governments in any negotiations that impact on devolved responsibilities. In Mark Drakeford's words, "We must be in the room."

He thought that this was no more than a matter of applying the current practice of having ministers from the devolved adminsitrations present when things such as agriculture, the environment or fisheries are discussed. This, he thought, was essential to the delivery of the next priority, "unambiguous continuation of devolved responsibilities." Scotland, Wales and Northern Ireland do not want repatriated powers in any area of currently devolved responsibilities to be shunted into sidings in Whitehall and Westminster. Instead, they should come direct to the devolved governments who could themelves decide whether any powers should be pooled anew.

On current evidence there will be some resistance to this non-Westminster presence from the UK Government and from MPs whose notions of Parliamentary sovereignty are still stuck in a pre-devolution era. This is why Mr Drakeford put forward a further priority – a commitment to re-drawing the relationship between the different parts of the UK. There are clearly concerns in Cardiff, Edinburgh and Belfast lest Brexit lead to a *de facto* re-centralisation of UK government. Post-Brexit, Westminster's hand will certainly feel heavier than Brussel's.

Mark Drakeford's final priority was as much a challenge to his fellow citiziens as to government. We are not leaving Europe, he said. But in order to preserve a powerful voice for Wales at the European level, Wales would need to be assiduous at all levels in involving itself in European networks. We would need to work hard to mobilise friends, particularly against the backdrop of Britain's reputation in Europe having been "curdled" by the Conservative Party.

There was no dissent from this list from the Plaid Cymru leader, Leanne Wood, who shared the platform. She thought there was no mandate for a 'hard Brexit'. Her emphasis was more on the need for a plan for Wales for the post-2020 period although, further ahead, the party's aim for renewed membership of the EU would remain.

It would not be unfair to characterise much of the debate as being about making the best of a bad job – minimising economic and social damage. One questioner asked whether the only way to achieve all these aims was to stay in the EU – in one sense a restatement of the view of the President of the EU, Donald Tusk, who has said that the only real choice is between hard Brexit or no Brexit. The question exposes the understandable nervousness of elected politicians of a Remain persuasion when faced with the suggestion of a further referendum. Although Mark Drakeford is an Assembly Member for a constituency in Cardiff – a city that voted more heavily for Remain than London – most Labour MPs and AMs and some of Plaid Cymru's MPs sit for constituencies that voted Leave, in some cases very heavily. Their dilemma is likely to be sharpened by Sir John Major's statement last week that there is "a perfectly credible case for a second referendum," and the predictable but ludicrous obloquy heaped upon him by outraged Brexiteers.

The case against even mentioning the possibility of another referendum at present is simply that it is still too close to the June event, that little is still known about the government's negotiating objectives, and not enough has changed since June in terms of broad public opinion, or according to some, objective economic circumstances. Remainers, not least those who are elected representatives, are very wary of any charge of acting undemocratically.

But Sir John – who has a cricket obsessive's sense of fair play – is right for other reasons. Through the referendum the Leave side has earned the right to seek satisfactory terms for our departure and a future arm's length relationship. But the closeness of the vote has not given it the right to impose any solution, regardless of the content and consequences of the deal. The complexity of the issues – economic, social and constitutional, not to mention peace and stability – meant that many voters on both sides of the argument will have felt considerable ambivalence while casting their votes. That is one basis for Sir John's warning against the 'tyranny of a majority'. For instance, many on the Leave side voted thinking that it would still be possible to stay in the single market and avoid adverse economic consquences. Many on the Remain side feared the economic consequences of leaving the EU while also harbouring many reservations about the union's structures and policies. For many the 52-48 split was there in different proportions within each person.

In June the country voted by a narrow margin to move house, without specifying what sort of house it was now looking for, or knowing what was available in other neighbourhoods, or even whether prices elsewhere were affordable. Meanwhile its bank manager told the nation last week that its bank balance was going to get worse, and there was fat chance of any improvement in its circumstances for the best part of a decade. He may not have been able to give us a totally reliable guide to our future earnings, but is helping us to fill out our own risk register. When things are clearer will we not want to ring the solicitor and tell him/her whether or not to proceed?

Now may not be the time to decide how the matter will be settled, but further down the line – in eighteen months or two years or three years – the whole country will be able to stand back and look objectively at its options. Our economy will have moved on, or backwards. The world will have moved on. We will know the shape of new governments in Germany, France, Italy and the Netherlands. We will have a better measure of the temper and policies of Preident Trump. We will know whether Vladimir Putin's preference is for continued provocation or a new prudence. We will have a better sense of an updated balance of risks, even if we do not all agree.

Adam Price,[13] while respecting the June outcome, made an important point at the conference about language. Talk of a second referendum ties a future event too closely to the one just gone. The next referendum, whose timing can only be dimly perceived, will be a different event. At the Swansea conference the sensible point was made that the vote to leave the European Union is just as important as the vote to join. It needs the same depth of detailed study

---

[13] Adam Price is the Plaid Cymru Assembly Member for Carmarthen East and Dinefwr and former MP for the same constituency.

by Parliament and, in all probability, the same degree of legitimation by the electorate. We should keep reminding ourselves of that fact.

## 20 January 2017

# Missive from May

Yesterday I received an unsolicited email from "Theresa May" setting out her Government's twelve negotiating objectives for leaving the European Union. She asked me to tell her what I thought about her plan. Never one to disappoint a searcher after truth, I thought I would oblige. I have a feeling this was not a private communication, so I am sure she will not mind if I share those thoughts with you.

Dear Theresa,

**1. Certainty.** You say you will provide certainty whenever you can and that any final deal will be put to a vote in both Houses of Parliament. You may have provided a little more clarity, but the uncertainty is going to persist well beyond the next two years during which we will be negotiating the terms of exit, not the details of a future deal.

As for the vote in Parliament, this is hardly going to be a free choice. It is more than likely that Pariament will be presented with a draft treaty that you will ask Parliament to accept or reject in its entirety. Aren't you going to be tempted to bully Parliament, too, into accepting the deal with the threat of no deal and an even worse outcome?

**2. Control of our own laws.** It is clear that you have prioritised the shibboleth of an old-fashioned, illusory sovereignty over the retention of real influence in a complex world. Britain would be better served by arguing – from the inside – for new procedures to enhance the role of national Parliaments within the EU.

**3. Strengthening the union.** Putting aside the referendum results in Scotland and Northern Ireland I was comforted, for a moment, by your reassurance that "the right powers", when repatriated, will be passed to the devolved administrations. That is, until I remembered Whitehall's mean-spirited approach to reserved powers, as expressed in the Wales Bill. Not a happy precedent. You won't find it easy to build unity in a poorer country.

**4. Maintain the Common Travel Area with Ireland.** Why do you take such a reductionist view of the dangers in Ireland – and at the very time that power-sharing in the North is going through a crisis. The truth is that the economies of the north and south are growing together and posterity will curse you if you make that more difficult.

**5. Control of immigration.** You say that you want to continue to attract 'the brightest and best' to work or study in Britain. You had a funny way of going about that as Home Secretary, refusing to take international students out of your immigration figures. It would be nice if you could bring yourself to mention the contribution of migrants to our public services.

**6. Rights for EU nationals in Britain and British nationals in the EU.** This is one area in which you could have made a positive gesture up front, and eased the pain of so many EU nationals in this country who have made their lives here and are deeply embedded in our communities. People should not be bargaining chips.

**7. Protect workers' rights.** I was glad that you said that workers' rights would be fully protected and maintained, but are you sure the rest of your party are with you on that? Everything that I have heard from your more rabid Brexiter colleagues talks about 'scrapping regulations'. Some, I am sure, would like a bonfire of them. I hope you will understand my scepticism.

**8. Free trade with European markets.** Interesting that you put this at number 8 in your list of priorities. Does that not tell us something? This really is the big 'cake and eat it' clause. I thought you said you did not want to be 'half in and half out', but you seem to want the free access we have now, plus bits of the customs union, as well as deals that look after the interests of the City, and the car industry, and aerospace – I could go on. Makes you wonder why we are leaving?

**9. New trade agreements with other countries.** I'm jolly glad you say you have "an open mind on how we achieve this end". You are going to need it. Seeing that Britain represents only 0.8% of the world's population, it takes some guts to walk out of a trading block that represents 7%, not to mention the trade deals that the EU already has with fifty countries across the world.

I know you are trying to cosy up to President Trump, but beware. One of his slogans was "Americanism not globalism". He is not going to do us any favours, much as he would like to annoy the EU. Take my advice, he will eat Liam Fox for breakfast.

**10. The best place for science and innovation.** It's clear that in this area you do want to be 'half in'. I suppose we should be grateful for that, considering what is at stake for our universities and the knowledge base of our industries. You would be amazed at just what the EU has meant for Welsh universities, both academics and students. I will write you again on that.

**11. Cooperation in the fight against crime and terrorism.** Yes, of course, but by now I'm beginning to think you want to be three-quarters in, not half in. Is there anything else you've missed? I'm confused.

**12. A smooth, orderly Brexit.** Apparently, you want agreement on our future partnership with Europe by the end of the Article 50 process, i.e. within the next two years. Given your shopping list, don't you think this is just a tad unreal. Have you forgotten the upcoming elections in the Netherland, France and Germany. That will mop up six months.

I know you consider any advice from Wales really carefully, so just a last word. As a serial optimist myself, I can spot another. We have a tendency to minimise difficulties. I know you want 'a global Britain', but Britain has not been very good at engineering economic miracles.

Since we have done our best to dismantle our manufacturing capacities over the last thirty years, we are going to struggle to rebalance our economy. Leaving ain't going to help.

It strikes me you prioritise political objectives over the economy. Don't be surprised if the rest of Europe wants to do the same. With Trump to the west and Putin to the east the whole of Europe has a lot at stake.

Best wishes. Sleep well.
Geraint

## 15 March 2017

# Single Market of the Mind[14]

The problem with analysing Britain's referendum on EU membership or, for that matter, any referendum, is that it can mean what you want it to mean. The teeming and lading of data and the dicing and slicing of arguments can be done by both sides, regardless of the result. And yet the result stands. Both sides are left dealing with consequences that were forecast or denied, hailed or howled down – a confusion of dreams and nightmares from which, in the harsh light of day, both the UK and our erstwhile partners in the EU now have to construct real solutions – separately or together. Without care and

---

[14] This is a summary of a report prepared for the Institute of Welsh Affairs. *Single Market of the Mind: Education and Culture in Wales after the Europe referendum*, Geraint Talfan Davies. IWA. 2017.

resolution, somewhere along the line it is certain that we shall bark our shins on the new realities.

For many of those who voted to Remain, as well as those from other EU countries who were not eligible to vote, the referendum result was a moment of emotional rupture. It was a blow to their sense of themselves as, simultaneously, citizens of their home country and of a wider continental entity. For others there was the prospect of a professional rupture, a direct impact on their working lives. Particularly in higher education and cultural spheres, collaboration across the boundaries of the EU has for long been an accepted part of working life, and an essential part too. For institutions there is the prospect of a rupture in funding sources and in the volume of funding, a rupture whose onset will become more visible over the next few years. Nowhere will this be felt more than in the university sector.

In the referendum the biggest single differentiator between Remain and Leave voters was educational qualification: 75% of those with no qualifications voted to leave, while only 27% of people with post-graduate degrees did so. This is not intended as a slight against those who voted Leave, rather as one stark measure of the divide in this country. It is no accident that the cultural sector was overwhelmingly supportive of our continued membership of the EU.

The UK is without question a world leader in higher education and in the arts and creative industries. That has been achieved in large part because we have been an intellectually open country with a high level of international engagement with peers in other EU countries. Sustaining this level of European engagement remains a vital national interest that has to be addressed constructively in any negotiation of our future relationship with the EU. It is of particular importance to universities outside the London/Oxford/Cambridge triangle, and more so to Wales than any other part of the kingdom. Higher education and cultural activity impact directly on the competitiveness and profile of Wales in the world. Whether we are in or out of the EU, the free exchange of ideas and talent will remain wholly necessary in both spheres. Wales has a lot at stake.

The issue is wider than funding alone, important though that is. It is also a matter of preserving unconstrained access to expertise and deep participation – by right as well as by inclination – especially in increasingly numerous formal European academic networks, often with connections to research and development by European companies. International collaboration is the name of the game in research. It has been estimated that in 1981 90% of UK research output was entirely domestic, whereas by now that domestic portion is down to one half, with almost all the growth in research over the last three decades attributable to international collaboration. The EU has been at the forefront of that, with the research budget increasing from a mere €3.3 billion in 1984-7 to €80 billion for 2014-20. By now 16% of academic staff in the UK are from other EU countries. At Swansea University, to take one example, there are one hundred and twenty-seven academic staff from other EU countries, twenty-seven of whom are at professorial level. At the same time, between 2007-13 four and a half thousand students and seven hundred and thirty-three staff from Welsh universities studied in other countries under the ERASMUS scheme that hopes to see twenty per cent of students spending some time abroad by 2020. The value, quality and intricacy of these connections will not be easily or satisfactorily sustained undamaged without continuing formal commitments by both the UK and the EU. Were the Welsh Government permitted 'red lines' in the negotiations, this would undoubtedly be one of them.

The world of the intellect knows no boundaries. Ideas cross boundaries with a speed our forebears could not have imagined. Educational, scientific and artistic collaborations already go well beyond the borders of the EU, and even if the UK withdraws from the EU, many working linkages will almost certainly survive. But in the last fifty years the EU has built a habit and depth of collaboration, and an intricacy of connections – intellectual, practical, financial, personal and professional. It is no longer a simple transactional arrangement, rather an evolving natural single market of the mind.

Any withdrawal from that single market of the mind poses a threat to the UK's research base, in a situation where our national investment in research and development is already significantly lower than that of many competitor countries. Our total research spend between 2008 and 2013 has grown by only 1.3%. The stark fact that emerges from all the data is that the UK's high performance in terms of research – the fifth largest producer of scientific and technical journal articles – is highly dependent on EU funding – much more so than other countries – because of the poor performance of both the UK government and British businesses in investing in R&D. The UK is twentieth in the world league table of

R&D spend as a percentage of GDP. That spend has dropped from 2.4% of GDP in 1981 to 1.63% today, considerably less than Germany's 2.85%. And yet, the UK is the second highest recipient of EU research funding over the decade 2006-15 – just behind Germany – and undoubtedly a net beneficiary. The ONS has calculated that in the period 2007-13 the UK contributed €5.4bn to the EU research funding pot but received €8.8bn back – a 63% return.

The threat to higher education in Wales and to the Welsh economy is disproportionately high. Across the UK EU funding represents roughly a third of the competitive funding distributed by the UK's Research Councils and Innovate UK. For Wales that EU funding represents nearly two thirds. In short, Wales has more to lose, and just at the wrong moment. In recent years the research record of Welsh universities has been on an upward trajectory, in both volume and quality. In quality terms the proportion of research at Welsh universities classified as 4* 'world leading' rose from 14% in 2008 to 30% in 2014. Volume is a bigger problem. At present we just don't have sufficient people working in high value research, particularly in science, technology, engineering, mathematics, and medicine. We are several hundred researchers short, although steps have been taken through the Welsh Government's £56m Ser Cymru II fund to plug that gap, with 51% of the money – £29m – coming from the EU. No less than £117m of research funding came into the HE sector in Wales from the EU during 2007-13, without counting the contributions from the ERDF that in recent years have amounted to £174m and which have funded major capital developments in almost every institution. Higher education has not been the only beneficiary. In further education the European Social Fund contributed £93m to fourteen projects during 2007-13.

The recent improvement in Wales' research performance has to be sustained over many years to come before we can be content that we have established a truly competitive quantum of R&D that can help close the gap with the rest of the UK in terms of economic performance. If the Welsh research effort is allowed to stall we will pay a high price.

There is just as much at stake in the cultural sphere. For a small country like Wales sport and culture play an unusually large role in defining its international profile. In the official sphere the Welsh brand can often struggle for visibility within the British envelope. But sporting teams carry the Welsh flag and the name as do many of our national arts organisations and individual performers when they operate within their traditionally international markets. Our film and television sectors rely more and more on international co-production, much of it with the USA but increasingly in recent years with Europe, especially now British audiences seem to have conquered their resistance to sub-titles. Other creative industries, especially new borderless digital industries such as video games, make extensive use of personnel from many countries and sell into worldwide markets.

In the cultural sector this international dimension starts with Europe. It does not exclude the rest of the world, but it starts with Europe not only because of proximity but also because we are part of the same shared civilisation stretching back over millennia. Much is made

– by British people especially – of the barrier of language within Europe, but language is only one facet of culture, important though it is. Each European country claims its own distinctiveness in language, culture, politics and institutions, but those distinct features are mostly woven from threads we share rather than existing in opposition to them. Europe is a continent shaped by Greek and Roman civilisations, with common roots in Christian, Jewish and, yes, even Muslim traditions. No language has borrowed more from other European languages than the English language, while over the centuries no European country's culture has been immune to the periodic movement of people – sometimes born of aggression, at other times persecution. English literature, French painting and German music are merely the more obvious examples of a shared kaleidoscopic heritage to which even a country as small as Wales has made its own unique contribution.

That being so, it is hardly surprising that no section of society was keener to retain membership of the EU during the recent referendum than the cultural sector. Various surveys registered support in the high nineties. This near unanimity was rooted not only in intellectual conviction but, for many organisations and artists, in the extent of their current international engagement. In this way higher education and the cultural sectors share a common view and interest – the need for internationalism and their investment in a world where ideas, good practice and people can travel without let or hindrance. Generally, practitioners have regarded artistic exchange and collaboration and the development of networks as much the most important aspect of their engagement with

Europe. Their main concern in the wake of the referendum has to do with the possible cultural impoverishment that might result from insensitive restrictions on freedom of movement and consequential additional costs.

In the cultural sphere, where Wales is deeply engaged internationally in many fields, quality has been enhanced by the absence of any unnecessary barriers to the free flow of ideas and talent. Whether it is Welsh National Opera co-producing with eleven other EU countries; or companies such as the National Dance Company of Wales or NoFit State Circus benefiting hugely from European talent, and touring regularly to EU-funded festivals; or Aberystwyth's Mercator Institute leading an EU-wide *Literature across frontiers* project; or our National Museum working with museum professionals from twenty-three EU states – our culture has been hugely enriched by that sense of a borderless community of art. That is why the cultural sector fears the return of clumsy and costly restrictions that it had thought were things of the past.

Whether in the field of university research, student and staff mobility, or in the artistic sphere, we will have to cope with three challenges: the threat to funding and to free movement, and the choice either of negotiating our continued access to the architecture of collaboration that the EU has built – the European Research Area, ERASMUS+ and Creative Europe – or of constructing new organisational structures of our own to develop and manage bilateral/multi-lateral arrangements that can have the same effect.

There are a number of lessons to be drawn from any study of this intense weave of European connections. First, that a hard Brexit could do untold damage to the educational and cultural fabric of Wales that would also harm our economic competitiveness. Second, these issues have to be a key part of any negotiation. Third, whatever the outcome, it is imperative that Wales creates a fuller more effective international strategy in which education, culture and the creative industries are essential components. Fourth, the pre-condition of any fully effective arrangements for the future is to know and understand the full extent of our current involvement with Europe in higher education, arts and culture, and what these connections have meant to both. That knowledge will show that 'global' is not an alternative to 'European', rather an extension of it.


## 25 April 2017

# Disenfranchising half the population

The UK's winner-takes-all electoral system is about to disenfranchise half the population on the most important issue the country has faced in half a century. If opinion polls are to be believed, this distorting prism will, in an unnecessary and unwanted General Election, turn a country evenly divided on the issue of our membership of the EU into a Parliamentary majority that could steamroller through any arrangement it desires regardless of the cost or consequences to us all.

Most likely pitted against the new government will be a weakened and divided Labour opposition that has a history of ambivalence on Europe, and where the be-grudgers have recently taken control against the wishes of the majority of its MPs, and virtually the whole of the party in Wales. At present, despite palpable discomfort with the Corbyn leadership, Keir Starmer is putting a brave face on it.

Labour will probably be joined on the opposition benches by a modest cohort of Liberal Democrats – a party that has a long, consistent and honourable record of support for the European ideal, has the clearest stance of any party on the issue, but which will be unable to stop the steamroller. Alongside them will be a loud SNP contingent – sincere in its Europeanism, but with other motives – and a small Plaid Cymru group of like mind, although with nothing to play for on the independence front. Meanwhile, on the probably swollen Conservative Government benches, we will have to watch for signs of a subterranean battle between cowed realists and crazed fantasists who are both on the same wrong train to a destination that currently neither can name or know. Ulster Unionists will be fellow travellers.

The misrepresentations of last year's referendum will be compounded by a government that will not hold back from misrepresenting the combined result of Labour's weakness and the country's weary fatalism as a vote of confidence in its own Brexit pig in a blue poke. This is at best an unedifying prospect for the whole country, and at worst potentially catastrophic. Small wonder that the 48% who voted to Remain are now canvassing democratic ways of massaging our clumsy electoral system in an attempt to create a Parliament that, at the very least, more accurately reflects the country's divided views. Electors need to know where their candidates – whether incumbents or challengers – stand, whether they were Remain or Leave, whether they will oppose the hard Brexit that is now most likely but for which the referendum offered no mandate, and whether Parliament or the country will have an opportunity to voice a further opinion on the matter. Wales for Europe will ensure that such information is available to all.

It will, no doubt, be more difficult to ascertain in what circumstances conscience will trump the instincts and the disciplines of party loyalty – an important matter in deciding how meaningful a Parliamentary vote on the outcome of negotiations will be. Beyond Parliament the history of tactical voting is not encouraging, but these are unprecedented times. All around the democratic world the talk is of 'insurgencies' and the election of 'outsiders'. Old party loyalties are dissolving, divisions of left and right are less meaningful. And on the issue of Europe, let's not forget that the extreme left and the extreme right often join hands.

Voters are unlikely to be much helped by the party manifestos. There is talk that the Conservative manifesto will be much shorter than in 2015, and will make fewer specific pledges. This is not some brilliant tactical ploy but an obvious necessity when we are at last two years away from knowing the outcome of any negotiations with the other twenty-seven member states. Until then we will have no idea of the extent of the damage to be incurred by our decision to disengage from our biggest trading partner, nor of its full impact on our economy or the public finances. Election manifestos could easily become so much waste paper.

During last year's referendum even leading Leavers had to acknowledge there would be damage. The only difference between the two sides was on just how much, and whether and on what timescale that damage could be repaired. Theresa May and Philip Hammond must be praying that in France on 7 May Emmanuel Macron bests Marine Le Pen.

Although Macron may insist on a tougher line in negotiations with the UK, a Marine Le Pen presidency could lead to a huge crisis for the French economy, and an existential crisis for the Euro and the EU as a whole – all of which would hit our economy too, redoubling the problems facing whoever is our Chancellor, not to mention every household in the land.

Polls are not yet showing much change on the Brexit issue, although the latest put Remain and Leave on level pegging. British *sang froid* and a lazy fatalism are still dominant. But worries are increasing. City firms are tossing up whether to go to Frankfurt or Paris. Two major EU agencies – the European Banking Authority and the European Medicines Agency – are set to leave London. Farmers, especially in Wales, are starting to worry that there may be no comfy replacement for the rug they pulled from under their own feet. Consumers are starting to face up to what Brexit-induced inflation means. President Trump has suddenly discovered that the EU is more important to the US than the UK. "Very important."

With fragility evident not just in the British economy but all around the world it defies belief that, even after a probable victory, Mrs May can lead this country through five full turbulent years – from 2017 to 2022 – without the people, rather than her, demanding that their voice be heard again.

## 30 May 2017

# Europe descends on Cardiff

The fact that the UEFA Champions League Final – one of the greatest events in the world's sporting calendar – is this week visiting the Welsh capital is a matter for pride and joy here at home: a time to show off Europe's youngest capital, another opportunity to demonstrate that Cardiff and Wales can punch well above their weight in mounting major events, whether sporting, cultural or political. It follows on from the hosting of a European Summit in the city in 1998 and, in neighbouring Newport, a Ryder Cup in 2010 and a NATO summit in 2014. Within a week of the Champions League leaving Cardiff, international singers will start to arrive for the BBC Cardiff Singer of the World competition.

And yet, many Welsh people will be conscious of an irony: that the Welsh capital has this week received its biggest ever influx of European visitors in the very year that the British Government has triggered the process of exiting from the European Union. Such irony is only redoubled by remembering that Wales's greatest footballing hero, the late John Charles, signed to play for Juventus in Turin (for a mere £65,000) in August 1957, only five months after the signing of the Treaty of Rome that created a European political and economic entity.

The post-war yearning for peace and the healing of wounds had many expressions, not just the creation of what was then the European Economic Community. 1947 saw the creation of the Llangollen International Eisteddfod in Wales and the Edinburgh Festival in

Scotland. UEFA itself dates from 1954 – less than a decade after the end of the war – at the prompting of Italian, French and Belgian football associations. It took another six years before the launching of the first European Cup in 1960.

Sport and culture can, of course, transcend political boundaries, even those of Europe itself. Today UEFA has fifty-five members that comprise not only the whole of the EU but also many countries beyond its borders in eastern Europe, including Turkey and Israel. Indeed, some of its members were once members of the Asian Football Confederation. But the countries of the EU are still its core – and in the case of the UK that means four countries – yet another reminder that, in practice, 'global' is not an alternative to 'European', rather an extension of it.

In the development of the EU itself even its leaders have often bemoaned the fact that it was built more from the top down than the bottom up. That may be true of the EU's institutions, but has that really been the case when the lives of European citizens are looked at in the round? Let us put aside for a minute our basic economic links – the five hundred firms from other EU countries that have operations in Wales, or the 190,000 Welsh jobs dependent on exports to the EU. It would be difficult to imagine nearly 200,000 European citizens descending on Cardiff for a weekend in any circumstances at any time before the last quarter of the 20th century. Post-war prosperity, the ease and cheapness of air travel and the building of the Channel Tunnel has created a European tourist industry in which we all participate frequently and with relish. Short city breaks in European cities hardly count any longer as 'going abroad'. A third of the EU's population will spend their main holiday in another EU country. Half of Wales's overseas visitors come from the EU. Many British holidaymakers will be more familiar with the beaches of Spain than those of Pembrokeshire. A British groom's stag party is now more likely to take place in Dublin, Paris, Amsterdam or Berlin than in the local pub – for which, often understandably, the host country does not always thank us. British cuisine is richer for its internationalisation, both European and Asian.

In television in the 1970s it was possible to argue that British viewers were more familiar with the streets of New York, Los Angeles or Dallas than with those of European cities. By now a new balance has been struck. Scandinavian, Italian and French drama series have eroded our resistance to sub-titles. It has also allowed Welsh language drama to reach a European audience.

In sport we have seen the Europeanisation of many sports, football most notably, but also rugby, although it has yet to make its mark right across the EU. The only problem has been that the importance of European competition for Welsh rugby followers has had to be measured, sadly, only by the extent of our disappointment at lack of success. Perhaps the difference is that rugby places a greater emphasis on country than on club, whereas in soccer those priorities are reversed – witness the scale of this UEFA Champions League final weekend.

In August next year this process of the Europeanisation of sport will take another step with the inaugural European Championships that will bring the existing championships of seven leading sports together into one coordinated event to be co-hosted by Glasgow and Berlin. This will include aquatics, cycling, gymnastics, golf, rowing and triathlon. The broadcasting partner is the European Broadcasting Union. Far from the image of the now overblown Olympics, one motive behind the initiative is to produce an affordable, sustainable event that does not need new stadia or athletes' villages, and which simultaneously raises the profile of European sport while sharing its costs. In sport as in so many aspects of life, Europe is already our rich and diverse backyard, and more of us have experienced more of it than in any previous generation.

The pity is that, over the last half century, while we have tempered the insularity of our island experience, we have not managed to temper the insularity of much of our politics. Instead too many British politicians have pointed our people away from the destination in which their lives were heading in so many other ways. So, for some of us, these festive days in Cardiff will be tinged with sadness. But *Wales for Europe / Cymru dros Ewrop* will remind our visitors that, despite everything, they will always be our European brothers and sisters.

19 June 2017

## Hard and Soft

*After much delay the negotiations between the UK and EU get under way.*

The Queen got it right – "It is difficult to escape a very sombre national mood". This is a joyless period for the country. Grief, fear, anger, disillusionment and, today, a strong sense that the Government is embarking on the most important negotiation in half a century in a state of muddle, uncertainty and weakness. When the EU's chief negotiator, Michel Barnier, sat down yesterday with David Davis, the Secretary of State for Exiting the European Union – a title that could be straight out of Gilbert and Sullivan – he may have learnt a little more than the British public knows at present. Quite what, we can only guess.

Why? Because the UK government's formal *public* position has not changed since it issued its 12-point statement last January; or if it has, it has been to adopt an even harder position. In January it was clear the Government was intent on having its cake and eating it. It wanted access to but not membership of the single market plus bits of the customs union, as well as deals that looked after the interests of the City, the car industry, aerospace, and our universities. It didn't want to pick cherries, it wanted to shovel them up.

But if its official position is publicly unchanged, its political brain must know that in the General Election on 8th June the electorate killed a hard Brexit stone dead as a political objective. There would be no Parliamentary majority for it. It would be opposed by all the devolved administrations. It would endanger the union in Scotland and peace in Northern Ireland. Yet as we speak, we know nothing of any formal change in the Government's objectives – despite the sharp rebuke from the electorate and despite the angry mood in the wake of the Grenfell Tower disaster, that has also killed the prospect of a low tax, regulation-lite Britain of which the more crazed Brexiteers dream.

In the last few days the UK has suddenly backed away from its insistence on dealing with the costs of the divorce and the separate issue of the content of a new deal in parallel. Instead, it has indicated that it is prepared to deal with the two matters sequentially, as the EU had requested. This is not some kind of clever last minute tactical move, but rather an indication that – with half David Davis's ministerial team having been sacked by Mrs May after the election – they have a desperate need for more time to agree on what sort of deal they want.

There has been a public assumption that the choice is between a hard or soft Brexit. The devolved administrations are all pushing for a soft one – even the DUP in Northern Ireland. Scotland and Wales never accepted Mrs May's original stance of prioritising the curbing of immigration over the interests of the economy. Neither did the bulk of British business. It wants jobs and the economy to be the top priority. But we need to remember two things: first, that a soft Brexit – this bowl of cherries – is not in our gift and, second, that hard and soft Brexits are not the only options. There is a third option – no Brexit. This elephant in not yet in the room, but it is loitering on the garden path.

In the General Election the country managed to derail the hard Brexit train. But there is no guarantee that we can lever a soft Brexit train onto the tracks. The assumption is that soft Brexit is an alternative option, but one cannot be confident of it. The Brexit lobby will threaten mayhem if anything like the Norwegian option comes into view. Norway contributes cash to the EU and obeys its trading rules, so getting full access to the EU market. It even allows free movement of people. But it gets no say in EU decisions. The EU, even if it wants to strike a deal with the UK, will not agree terms that are equal to those we have as a full member. Countries have both economic and political objectives. That also applies to the EU.

At some point in the next eighteen months, the gap between the benefits of our current EU membership and any deal on offer will become clear and, perhaps for the first time, measurable. Or it will become clear that no deal is possible. If it becomes clear that a soft Brexit is unachievable or unsatisfactory and that a hard Brexit is still unacceptable, that will be the point at which the third option – no Brexit – will thrust itself forward.

Do not expect public opinion to be static in the next two years. British politics is in a precarious and febrile state. Although many in the Conservative party would dearly wish to keep yet another general election at bay, Theresa May's hapless performance over the last week does not suggest that will be possible. Labour may relish the prospect of power, but if that were to come about it is its own internal divisions on the European issue that will come to the fore. Although shares in Corbyn have risen sharply, it should not be forgotten that the ambivalence of both Jeremy Corbyn and John McDonnell on the issue during the referendum was, arguably, of material and perhaps decisive help to the Leave cause.

Brexiters, on the other hand, are advancing the completely specious argument that in the General Election eighty-four per cent of voters voted for two parties arguing to Leave. I say specious, because our 'first-past-the-post' electoral system, and the high prevalence of tactical voting means it is impossible to be categorical about the wishes of the electorate on a single issue. Brexiters also argue that half the Remain vote is now in favour of Leave. Again, that is far too simplistic. People have not so much changed their minds, they have just been worn down by poor and repetitive debate during three major campaigns in three years. They just want it all to stop. I'm afraid it's not going to.

## 30 July 2017

# Mixed signals

As the UK Government chokes on an American chlorinated chicken, the stance of Her Majesty's Opposition is undoubtedly a matter of some importance. One might have thought that clarity on its part would have assumed a higher priority. Not so, it seems. At the very moment when a rapier thrust – into the chicken or the Fox – would have done maximum damage, several of its leaders have seemed intent on pinning a target on themselves instead. Mr Corbyn, never strong on footwork, was asked three times by Andrew Marr a week ago whether he would like to see the UK leave the single market. Mr Corbyn said we had no choice but to leave because "the single market is dependent on membership of the EU." Within minutes a queue of people formed to tell Mr Corbyn that this was not true. Norway, Lichtenstein and Iceland participate in the single market, without being members of the EU.

He was more equivocal about remaining part of the EU customs union, unlike his own shadow Trade secretary, Barry Gardiner, whose article in *The Guardian* ruled out both the customs union and the Norway model that, he said, would reduce us to 'a vassal state'. No hedging there. Contrary to the views of Mr Corbyn and Mr Gardiner, the Welsh First Minister, Carwyn Jones, was categorical that "there is no need to leave the single market even as we leave the EU." In this he has been admirably consistent. Mr McDonnell, while touring Pembrokeshire last week, took the view that these labels do not matter – we can sort out a deal and decide how to label it afterwards. It makes you wonder why Keir Starmer, the man who actually holds the European brief in the Shadow Cabinet did not take the offer of a job with a London law firm. No wonder he always looks as if he is about to burst into tears.

The truth is that this is slippery ground. It is not easy for the public, or even avid students of these matters, to distinguish clearly between being 'a member of' or 'having access to' or 'participating in' the single market. The distinction between the single market and the customs union is somewhat clearer, although most members of the public will still dismiss it as an arcane matter. That said, the single market and the customs union are undeniable realities. They have and will continue to have form and substance. Leaving them will have profound consequences.

A plea in mitigation for Labour's seeming confusion would run as follows. The Labour Party cannot afford to be too categorical at this stage. It also wants to win an election. To do so, it cannot afford to be seen to push the public prematurely towards a rejection of the EU referendum result, however qualified. It may, however, be willing to be pulled in this direction once there is unequivocal evidence that public opinion has taken fright at the prospect of Brexit. If it is not to exacerbate division in the country it will need to count a few more chlorinated chickens first.

If this is really the situation, then one might have expected someone to have told the Shadow Trade Secretary, or to have suggested a few more deft words for Mr Corbyn to utter. Surely, it is high time Mr Corbyn said something warm about Europe and its values. He might also like to contrast those values with the bleak idiocies emanating from Washington. The question that hangs in the air is this: are Jeremy Corbyn and his Shadow Chancellor, John Macdonnell, really trapped by their tactical caution and a necessary public respect for the referendum result or, rather, by their past long-standing hostility to the EU? The belief that the latter constraint is the stronger factor is buttressed by knowledge of the ideological stance of unelected members of their inner team.

It could be that these doubts will be put to the test sooner than we think. After all, nothing is currently moving smoothly for the UK Government. Its leader, far from being an iron lady, is holed below the waterline. Her government is struggling both to arrive at a coherent position and to cope with the sheer scale of the Brexit agenda. We all know that it is not just a tactical disagreement that separates Mr Hammond from Mr Fox. The internal, ideological divisions in Mrs May's party are ultimately far deeper than those within Labour. Her government, too, is not above creating semantic problems for the public to unravel: ending 'freedom of movement' (the legal requirement), as stated by the Immigration Minister, Brandon Lewis, will not apparently mean ending 'freedom of movement' (the practice) as enunciated in the same twenty-four hours by the Home Secretary, Amber Rudd. The public is also asked to divine the difference between 'a transitional period' and 'an implementation period'.

The most serious import of the Chancellor's latest intereview on the BBC's *Today* programme is that the UK will leave the EU in March 2019, and that a two to three year period will be needed not so much to *implement* an agreement already arrived at – i.e to transition – but actually to complete the negotiation. It was, in fact, a confirmation that if we leave in March 2019 it will be for a destination still undefined.

The difference between Mr Hammond and his more rabid colleagues is that while they are panting for a giant leap into the dark, he would prefer a gentle slide into the gloom, despite knowing full well that Brexit will make it doubly difficult to find any route out of austerity for a tired and dispirited country. Please note that gentle slide will be *after* our exit. These are degrees of darkness.

It makes it even more difficult to understand why Labour does not take a more robust pro-European line. What's the blockage? Internally, unlike the Conservatives, the party does not have to manage a large, practiced and shouty cohort of fanatical anti-Europeans – quite the contrary. Externally, current evidence points to a large majority of Labour voters favouring Remain. The young are overwhelmingly for Labour and for Europe. Labour's influence in the next twelve months will be decisive. In that time we shall discover whether, on Europe, the reasons for nervousness about Mr Corbyn and a more visceral distrust of Mr Macdonnell will be scotched or re-doubled.

## 30 August 2017

# Battle lines become clearer

Perhaps we should learn to fear August. It's a bad month. The Houston floods and North Korea's missile over Japan are merely this year's contribution to a catalogue of August events that include the start of the First World War, the first and second military use of atomic bombs, Iraq's invasion of Kuwait and the beginning of the Berlin Wall – not to mention the deaths of Marilyn Monroe, Elvis Presley and Princess Diana. Still, it's almost over.

Against this cataclysmic historical backdrop the Labour Party's apparent edging towards continued membership of the EU's single market and customs union might seem small beer. After all it would be easy to knock it: too little, too late, hardly epoch-making; no certainty past a transition period; the suspicion of a tactical move rather than deep-seated conviction. And yet, and yet, it is movement. And one that strangely mirrors that of its opponents. Just as a riven UK Government has shuffled towards recognising the need for a transition period, and has even tipped its hat to the European Court of Justice, the Labour Party seems now to have hung its hat on the peg of the single market and customs union. The increased distance between the two main parties, and the welcome sense of battle more clearly joined, makes it easy to miss the fact that in both parties the direction, though not the distance of travel, is the same. Both are bowing to the realities.

But having breathed a sigh of relief, we then have to hold our next breath. For though Labour has moved further than the government, one does not yet know how fully Messrs Corbyn and Macdonnell have suppressed, and will continue to suppress, their long-standing personal hostility towards Europe. They are not a duo who are likely to proclaim anything more than the transactional benefits of a European union.

For the moment, let's give credit where it is due. For months Keir Starmer, the Shadow spokesman on Europe, has seemed a tortured soul. His discomfort has been palpable. He has faced the painful necessity of having to rein in his own party leaders before fixing his sights on the opposition. But he has succeeded, maybe partially, but to an important degree. The main UK opposition party has now put clear water between itself and a government hemmed in by its own disunity and downright fear of the Europhobe extremists in its Cabinet and on its backbenches.

No-one will be more relieved at Labour's shift than the Welsh Government. Too often, even when on the same stage, Carwyn Jones and Jeremy Corbyn have rarely given the impression of being on the same page. This has been an embarrassment for Labour at both ends of the M4, although more keenly felt at this end. We now have a situation where Labour, SNP, Plaid Cymru, the Liberal Democrats and the Green Party are all in favour of our continued membership of the single market. There is now no reason for them not to collaborate closely in the debates and votes on the EU Withdrawal Bill in order to fend off any notion of a hard Brexit that would do untold damage to the economy, not least in Wales where we are in no position to take more hits. There will be a lot to fight for this autumn and through 2018. Where this country will end up may depend on the convictions and tactical astuteness of the Labour leadership as well as the speed with which three different but parallel narratives unfold.

First, there is the passage of the European Union (Withdrawal) Bill, and other Brexit-related legislation, during which there is now a better chance of engineering some rebellion from amongst the one hundred and seventy-six current Tory MPs who voted Remain. Astute tactical judgment will still be required to stave off the harder options, to ensure that Parliament not the executive remains in control of any post-Brexit legislative process, and to prevent the rolling back of devolution through the reassertion of an outdated English centralism. The stumbling blocks are large. One can easily foresee stalemate in either the British Parliament or in the Brussels talks, or both? Could another general election intervene?

Second, there is the progress of the negotiations, where it is impossible to predict what degree of compromise or implacability will be permitted by twenty-seven countries anxious to preserve a union whose continuation is vital to their interests (just as it is to ours, whether we are in or out). Third, there are the unfolding economic consequences of the referendum decision – not least, the impact on the pound, by now indelibly imprinted on the credit card bills of every British holidaymaker in Europe. We are all, already, poorer. Even the most rabid leavers accept that things are likely to get worse for Britain before they get better.

These parallel narratives may unfold at different speeds, posing another question. Will the probable negative economic consequences be sufficient to change public opinion before, or only after, we have left the EU? That last question is important because, for many Remain MPs, a shift in public opinion is the pre-condition for demanding that the matter be put back to the British people. This is why there should be a new urgency in the work of all the pro-EU forces in the country, and effective collaboration to fight any incipient fatalism in a country wearied by prolonged austerity. We must continue to remind every part of our society – our businesses, our farmers, our universities and students, our public services, and our communities, urban and rural – that this process is a massive and destructive distraction for the whole country, imposing an opportunity cost that will entail lost jobs, lost influence and lost decades, and blighting the future of a whole generation in the process.

24 September 2017

## May at the Gates of Paradise

Some months ago I made the incontrovertible claim that Brexiters were trying to sell us a pig in a poke. To my surprise I was asked by some people what 'pig in a poke' meant. A poke being an old word for a small sack, the phrase means buying something without knowing its value. This surprising unfamiliarity with what was once a very common saying in our language is the only reason why I am nervous in saying of Mrs May's Florence speech that fair words butter no parsnips.

I have no doubt that Mr Jacob Rees-Mogg would be able to tell you the meaning of both phrases. For all I know, he may even be able to tell you their Latin equivalents. But, despite his instant criticism of his Prime Minister's speech as an incipient sell-out of the Brexit cause, he is wrong if he thinks that she buttered any Remain parsnips – true though it is that she has had to take note of her own Chancellor's greater realism and to concede that we will need time to unravel more than forty years of constitutional and commercial knitting together of our European partnership. Given the snail's pace at which discussions have proceeded so far, as well as the time needed for ratification of any deal by twenty-seven countries, the likelihood is that March 2019 will prove an impossibly tight deadline.

As Prime Minister of a country that makes much of the rule of law and as a person who presumably subscribes to Anglican codes of behaviour Mrs May has also recognised our obvious legal and moral obligations to pay our EU bills until 2020, and maybe beyond – something she could have done months ago. No-one believes that the mooted £20 billion is anything other than a starting figure in the negotiations. That said, she is still unable to paint even the haziest picture of what our future relationship with the EU will be. The future for Britain remains clouded in uncertainty and fraught with danger.

There are many phrases in the speech that seem to acknowledge those dangers, though without following through their logic. Let her speak for herself:

"Here on our own continent, we see territorial aggression to the east; and from the south threats from instability and civil war; terrorism, crime and other challenges which respect no borders... The only way for us to respond to this vast array of challenges is for likeminded nations and peoples to come together and defend the international order that we have worked so hard to create – and the values of liberty, democracy, human rights and the rule of law by which we stand."

It could have come from a speech by the late Roy Jenkins, the one British President of the European Commission. And again: "Mass migration and terrorism are but two examples of the challenges to our shared European interests and values that we can only solve in partnership." She even conceded that "the profound pooling of sovereignty that is a crucial feature of the European union permits unprecedentedly deep cooperation, which brings benefits." Amen to that.

But against that she pitched two arguments: first, that within the EU "when countries are in a minority they must sometimes accept decisions they do not want". And, second, that "the United Kingdom has never totally felt at home being in the European Union...perhaps because of our history and geography the European Union never felt to us like an integral part of our national story."

As for the first of these arguments, it hardly squares with the fact that that between 2004 and 2009 the UK voted on the majority side in the Council of Ministers 97.4% of the time. Even in the period 2009-15, mostly under a Conservative government struggling with its own internal divisions, the UK was on the majority side in the Council of Ministers on 86.7% of occasions. In this latter period a high proportion of the dissenting occasions were to do with budgetary policies and foreign and security matters, rather than on trade, industry, environment, transport or legal affairs.

And as for 'not feeling totally at home' in Europe or Europe 'not being an integral part of our national story' – this leaves out of account profound changes in the ease and cost of transport and travel in Europe as well as shared cultural consumption, sporting endeavour and research collaboration. At a deeper level it also leaves out of account ways in which the reality of cross cultural influences and Britain's involvement in European history differs from the story we, or rather our media, have chosen to tell ourselves. It is truly symbolic that arch-Brexiter, Nigel Lawson, opines on the European issue from his mansion in Armagnac.

Taken together, it leaves one wondering what on earth Mrs May believed when, apparently, she cast her vote for Remain last year. Did she flip a coin? In Florence she stated baldly that "we can't leave the EU and have everything stay the same." No-one will quarrel with that, but one might expect our Prime Minister to be able to tell us what will be different. Equally baldly, she said "we will no longer be members of its single market or its customs union." Now that is a very big difference indeed. It is also a statement that, quite apart from its likely economic consequences, puts her immediately at odds with the Welsh and Scottish Governments, as well as creating jeopardy for Northern Ireland.

In a further sentence that combines ambition, banality and zero substance this rather uncreative politician urged negotiators to be "creative as well as practical in designing an ambitious economic partnership which respects the freedoms and principles of the EU, and the wishes of the British people". Her own creative juices brought forward no hint of how these things might be squared. Perhaps she is waiting for a re-born Florentine sculptor to carve her the Gates of Paradise anew. But in arguing that these things cannot be squared – that you cannot have your cake and eat it – there is one caution here for those of us who have opposed Brexit, including the Welsh Government. The implication is that, in the end, there will be no choice other than between a hard Brexit and no Brexit. At best, any Brexit will be more hard than soft. In this situation the case for No Brexit must not go by default. That will be the next stage in the debate.

## 11 November 2017

## A boxful of conundrums

In the saga of Britain's stuttering negotiations over Brexit, one senses that we are coming to another crunch point. M. Barnier, and the twenty-seven EU countries he represents, want clarity from the UK on a number of issues within the next two weeks. He is not the only one. The British public need and deserve clarity too. But don't hold your breath.

This is a government of fractious children playing with a toy set that came with no careful instructions. They cannot even refer to a handy drawing on the cover of the box. There is a prevailing sense that David Davis's meaningless repetitions at EU press conferences, far from being elements in the strategy of a brilliant poker player, are simply a sign that that he himself and the Government as a whole have no idea where they are heading. By now it is a government clearly overwhelmed by the complexity of it all – the boxful of conundrums that it faces – and the knowledge that it lacks any political force or authority sharp enough – if I may change the metaphor – to slice through this daunting row of Gordian knots.

Even if intent on leaving the EU, the rational thing to have done nine months ago would have been to confess to the scale of the task, to have sought more time to think and to develop a considered position, and not to have triggered Article 50 when it did. Instead the government started the clock running on a time period that was not open ended. As the former foreign secretary, David Miliband, said in another flourish of metaphors at the weekend: "The triggering of Article 50 was so monstrously premature. We're sitting on a grenade with the pin pulled out. I don't see any rainbow at the end of this."

As if to compound the mistake, still with no solution in sight, the government now seeks to set in statute a time and date for our departure from the EU – 1100 GMT, 29 March 2019 – with farcical precision. Given the current pace of negotiations it beggars belief that we will, by that chime of the clock and on that day, have negotiated a deal, had it approved in "a meaningful vote" in Parliament, and had it ratified by the Governments and legislatures of twenty-seven other countries as well as by the European Parliament. It is obvious to all who have eyes to see that Mrs May has had to set this legislative alarm clock, at the behest of those in her government who are running scared lest an utterly essential transition period become sensibly prolonged and, particularly, lest the British electorate should begin to change its collective mind. This is what comes of having a core of Ministers who, believing that the UK has a set of magic wings, would be perfectly happy to see no deal at all, at which point we would launch ourselves from the cliff edge. These are people of such tested sagacity as Priti Patel and Boris Johnson, to name but two.

And yet we are asked to believe such people when they tell us that having departed the EU fold, we can put our faith in the benign altruism of President Xi and President Trump. Liam Fox, clad in Britannia's shining breastplate, tells us he will see off all-comers. In Mr Fox's personal interest there should be an early appeal to the British Boxing Board of Control. If you want to judge in which weight category we should be placed don't look at forecasts, look at the most recent statistics, since the past is usually a fair guide to the future. In 2016 total EU exports to China amounted to €169 billion. Of that Germany accounted for €77 billion, while the UK managed only €16 billion. In the same year total EU exports to the United States amounted to €362 billion, of which Germany accounted for €107 billion, and the UK €54 billion. To set out these figures is not to do Britain down, it is simply to describe the world as it is. If nothing else, do these figures not tell us, pretty accurately, and putting all personalities aside, where the priorities of the world's two economic giants will lie? What is at stake here is not national pride, but the jobs of people at Airbus and Tata and Ford, just to name three of the five hundred companies from other EU countries that have operations in Wales.

The other issue that is concerning the EU, and particularly the Irish Government is the issue of the border between Northern Ireland and the republic – what would be, post Brexit, the UK's only land border with the EU. What is it that this government does not understand about the dangers for Northern Ireland, and for the unity of the UK? The EU has been a framework in which the nations of the UK could finesse their differences and in which thirty years of terrorism was defeated: a government context that helped dismantle economic and military barriers around Ulster, and allowed devolution in Scotland, Wales and Northern Ireland an enabling breadth that might not survive the centralist restrictions of the EU Withdrawal Bill.

In the case of Ireland no-one on either side of the current negotiation has come up with a realistic way of squaring this circle: how can the UK leave the customs union without recreating a border that has caused generations of grief? Ideas proferred by British negotiators have ranged from the constitutionally problematic to the technically fanciful. God forbid that British carelessness should fan any lingering embers of violence back into life.

3 December 2017

# Brexit's huge opportunity cost

Public opinion on Brexit is a mystery. It can only be because a large part of the British public has 'tuned out' from the debate. This surely cannot last. For underlying the reluctance to revisit the issue lies a deep pessimism about the consequences. According to YouGov more people now think Britain was wrong rather than right to vote Leave, although the gap is not huge. But far more now think we will be worse off, rather than better off; that the effect on jobs and the NHS will be bad rather than good, and that we will have less rather than more influence in the world. An overwhelming majority (64/21) think the government is handling the negotiations badly. Is Britain really so psychologically flawed that it would persist in what it knows to be self-harm? Or is it, surely, only a matter of time before this already deeply negative perception of Brexit translates into calls for a change of course?

The resignation of every member of the government's commission on social mobility this weekend because, faced with Brexit, the government 'does not have enough band-width' to deal with the problem, is but one sign of the opportunity cost that the Brexit obsession is imposing on the country. This cost is measurable. Mr. Hammond is choosing to spend £3 billion in two years on Brexit preparations, more than the extra money promised to the NHS. Expenditure on the UK civil service will be £2.1 billion higher than expected in 2019-20. Amber Rudd, the Home Secretary, is having to hire twelve hundred immigration officials simply to register the three million EU nationals that have been living and working securely in this country, sharing, as we all do, in the beautiful reality of a common European citizenship.

Far from giving us back control, the mere prospect of Brexit is already reducing our capacity to tackle our own problems, and will do so increasingly as it bites on the economy and the public finances. While our real problems are serious and legion – individual and regional inequalities, poverty, education, health and social care, low investment and low productivity – the Brexit debate has swamped the news and the government. Even on that subject we have had repetitive and insubstantial exchanges between the British Minister, David Davis, and the EU's lead negotiator, Michel Barnier. The listener is soon engulfed in a cloud of generalities from Mr Davis, counterpoised by M. Barnier's contained exasperation, conveyed 'more in sorrow than in anger'. Mr Davis's cheeky chappy routine is wearing thin. Meanwhile, back at Westminster, ministers negotiate with each other, sometimes in public, about how hard or soft a stance Britain should take. It is an unedifying process that leaves the public in the dark, either comatose or wearily suspicious.

No doubt Mr Davis would argue this is inevitable, given the nature of negotiation and the seriousness of what is at stake in these discussions. This cannot all be played out in public. Maybe. But the shambles over the publication of the British Government's Brexit background papers – allegedly fifty-eight of them – does not create any faith in the competence or honesty of Ministers. If there is a cunning plan, it is more probably of the sort conjured by the ineffable Baldrick. Our Foreign

Secretary has said that the EU can 'go whistle' for any money to settle the divorce, yet this week we learn that at least £50 billion is on the table although we are also asked to believe that no figures at all have been mentioned. The more swivel-eyed Brexiters are already threatening to vote down any deal because of this, preferring to ditch our obligations and jump from the cliff edge with pockets bulging and Britain's integrity and honour in tatters.

Some while back Mrs May was telling us that 'no deal would be better than a bad deal'. Now she is arguing for "a deep, special and comprehensive relationship with the EU". Some of us will argue that is precisely what we have had for the last forty-three years, and that any deal arrived at in the next twelve months cannot be as deep, as special or as comprehensive as the one we will now pay £50 billion and more to get out of. But, on the admittedly now shaky assumption that words mean something, what is that 'deep, special and comprehensive' arrangement that she now seeks? On the further assumption that any new deal will be less than the status quo, what is it that she is prepared to junk? Is it of such insignificance that she can discard it without damaging the 'comprehensiveness' of the arrangement? When is comprehensive less than comprehensive?

When might Mrs May share the identity of these apparently junkable trifles with the governments of Scotland and Wales? Have they a lesser right to this information than Northern Ireland's DUP, whose stance on Europe, strangely, seems to draw no criticism from the London press despite being contrary to the democratic wish of the province to remain in the EU. It is remarkable that so far in 2017 Mrs May has seen a lot more of the DUP leader, Arlene Foster, who – to reverse a famous phrase – is in power but not in office, than of the elected leaders of Scotland and Wales who govern fifteen per cent of the population of this land. What possible explanation can there be of the fact that a plenary session of the Joint Ministerial Committee – created to bring together the heads of central and devolved governments – has not met since last January, and this during a period of existential importance to all. A nasty question looms. Is this how the UK will work once we have left the European Union – a reassertion of the defining deafness of the central power?

The shortage of bandwith is also excluding issues of vital importance to Wales: the vulnerability of Welsh farming, whose representatives are becoming increasingly alarmed; the vulnerability of our automotive sector, where Ford managers have warned that a hard Brexit could see the company taking a £1 billion hit; the future of Airbus, where other EU countries are already eyeing the wing production line at Broughton that alone accounts for a significant chunk of Welsh GVA.

Notwithstanding the still unsolved conundrum of the Ulster border, if, as Brexit optimists tell us, we are about to move on from the heads of terms for a divorce into substantive negotiations on a new deal, are the governments of Scotland and Wales to be kept in the dark about the key elements that the UK side is seeking? The UK government may not grant Scotland and Wales a veto over any deal – though obviously readier to grant Northern Ireland that privilege – but it might like to listen to common sense from two First Ministers who seem rather closer to their people.

## 14 December 2017

# Brexit roller-coaster

*Parliament starts to flex its muscles, and the Government suffers its first major defeat.*

It has been a extraordinary week on the Brexit roller-coaster, culminating in the government's first Parliamentary defeat. Defeat from the jaws of victory. Victory from the jaws of defeat. Take your pick, according to taste and the day of the week. But stable it ain't. A week ago Mrs May, bleary-eyed, recovered from the earlier snarling DUP spoiler to clinch a pre-breakfast deal with the EU on the terms of divorce. The gung-ho headlines in the tabloid press were predictable. The *Daily Mail's* "We're on our way" – the writer having failed to notice that the headline can be read two ways – was supposedly designed to raise a cheer. It may not have noticed that cheering was nowhere to be heard. While a grudging DUP continued to make grumpy noises in the background, and Mr Farage does what Mr Farage does, Michael Gove went into overdrive, showering Mrs May with praise on the BBC's *Today* programme, even while scribbling an article for the *Daily Telegraph*, telling its readers that "If the British people dislike the arrangement... the agreement will allow a future government to diverge."

Not to be outdone, the following day Brexit Secretary, David Davis, told Andrew Marr on his Sunday show that the agreement was merely a 'statement of intent' rather than legally enforceable. Under pressure from furious colleagues and Brussels he attempted to take it all back on Monday. It followed hard on the heels of his denial to a Parliamentary Committee of the existence of 'impact assessments' – or should one say 'sectoral analyses' – that he had previously told them existed in 'excruciating detail'. No doubt his department will soon be renamed the Department for Exiting Any Statement. By the end of the week he had only narrowly avoided being charged with contempt of the House.

There was a time when Britain had a reputation for 'fair play' and 'doing the right thing'. Perhaps that reputation was never wholly deserved. All countries tend to pursue their own interests, and hypocrisy has ever been a deniable tool of statecraft. But it would have been nice had this dysfunctional government managed not to destroy all trust even before the ink was dry on our withdrawal agreement with the EU – an agreement the government had initially asked us to applaud. How can anyone negotiate with a government that seems unable to hold a steady line for more than five minutes. No wonder M. Barnier, who does *hauteur* even in the good times, and Mr Verhofstadt for the European Parliament started to insist on having the deal in joined-up writing, if possible on parchment with lashings of sealing wax.

If there weren't so much at stake one might dismiss it all as a theatrical mish-mash of *The Thick of It* and old-fashioned Whitehall farce. But the shambles had consequences. The mistrust sown at the start of the week became a crucial ingredient in deciding the outcome of the debate on Wednesday. In the end Conservative rebels simply did not trust their own government to do the honourable thing, and the Commons passed Amendment

7 to the European Withdrawal Bill that, if it survives the rest of the Parliamentary obstacle race, will ensure that MPs get the nearest thing to a 'meaningful vote' that people seem capable of imagining at present. Given the slim majority of four (309-305) the quartet of Plaid MPs were quick to deluge social media with claims that they made the difference. (Shades of the 1970s). Predictably, the government responded with the bad grace for which it is becoming known, threatening to remove the offending amendment at a later stage.

One can but suppose that senior members of the Cabinet believe they have this licence to go freelance, not only because of Mrs May's weak position but also because the government has no settled collective position on what it wants to achieve in the more important negotiations on the substance of our future relationship with Europe.

The problem is exacerbated by the caveat in the withdrawal agreement that "nothing is agreed until everything is agreed". God knows how long that will be. The earliest possible date is currently set at 29 March 2019, the planned date of our withdrawal, only fifteen months away. Yet the best we are likely to achieve by then is a 'framework agreement'.

If this year's slow trudge to an agreement on the mere preliminaries of our withdrawal from the EU has taught the government one thing, it is surely that time and circumstance are not on its side. Nine of the twenty-four months allotted under Article 50 have elapsed, squandered on those preliminaries. If the government wants to stick to its plan to leave the EU on 29 March 2019 – and the Conservative rebels might even manage to expunge that from the Bill – far from having fifteen months left to negotiate the framework agreement, it has only another nine or ten months.

As for circumstance, it is surely clear that this is and will continue to be an unequal fight. There is a massive gap between the UK and the EU in terms of clarity of objective, negotiating firepower, depth of preparation, and sheer numbers: population, size of market and economic clout. Those who argue that "they need us as much as we need them" are clearly not good at sums. Those multiple disparities are going to be even more in evidence when talks begin on the infinitely more time-consuming work of negotiating the endless minutiae of trade in what, to use David Davis's own words, will be "excruciating detail". Those details will haunt him for as long as he is in office, and they will matter to the lives of everyone of us for a lot longer.

On one thing government ministers are right: the passing of Amendment 7 does not, of itself, mean that Brexit will not happen. But it does represent another of those small movements – that include changes in public opinion and in the mutating stance of the Labour leadership – that mean nothing can be ruled out.

23 December 2017

## Passport pantomime

Can anything speak louder about the current puerile state of British government thinking than the trumpeted news of its intention, in a fit of induced pre-Brexit nostalgia, to issue new dark blue passports rather than the current burgundy-coloured document that has been issued to us all for the past thirty years? Three days before Christmas, as charities tended to the ballooning numbers of homeless sleeping in the streets, Mr Brandon Lewis, a Home Office minister who was only seventeen when the last 'blue' passports were issued under the name of Her Britannic Majesty, felt it necessary to command the airwaves to announce this gift to a pining nation, complete with a manufactured lump in his throat.

Ah! He and his colleagues must have known they have been talking of little else in Pontypridd or Llanfairfechan for the past thirty years. The change of colour in 1988 was, according to one Brexiter MP, 'a national humiliation'. If a nation can be humiliated by such a paltry change, it must suffer from very low self-esteem. According to another MP, presumably colour blind, the current passport is 'pink' which, we must presume, he deems an insult. Read into that what you will. But if there has been wailing and gnashing of teeth and a rending of garments on the streets of Penarth or Penrhiwceiber all these years, we must all have missed it.

Anyone under fifty – apart, that is, from Mr Brandon Lewis – must wonder what the fuss is about. Anyone outside Britain, sufficiently careless of their own time to pay attention, must wonder why the men in white coats have not been sent for. On cue, Mr Nigel Farage, tells us "You can't be a nation unless you have this symbol", an assertion that wipes out rather a large chunk of our history, since the first modern British passports were not issued until after the passing of the British Nationality and Status Aliens Act in 1914, and the blue one did not surface until 1920. I might conceivably understand if, in previous centuries, the select few who were granted a safe conduct letter from the monarch went dewy-eyed as they clutched the royal missive. But in the 21$^{st}$ century? No passport, no nation? Really.

Perhaps, on Mr Farage's next visit to Trump Tower, Mr Trump will remind him that only forty-six per cent of Americans own a passport without, apparently, any diminution in the patriotism of the bereft fifty-four per cent. Indeed, Mr Trump might also boast – uncharacteristically accurately – that there is a striking correlation between the states that voted for him and the states with the lowest numbers of passport holders.

No doubt people will accuse me of a lack of emotional intelligence if I fail to appreciate the importance of a passport's colour, but the weakness of the argument is proven by considering the reverse proposition: let's get rid of a dull inky blue-black document, a million miles from royal blue, and replace it with a rich and regal burgundy colour that represents that very large part of France over which English kings once ruled. Absurd, but it is the kind of proposition that might easily have emerged from, say, Mr Jacob Rees-Mogg. The real import of this holiday season row is to emphasise the shallowness of this government in believing that the colour of a passport is a matter that exercises the nation and that could distract it from the pain caused by current levels of austerity, inequality and crying social need.

There is only one issue of substance raised by the prospect a new passport after 29 March 2019, and that is what is implied by the removal of the words European Union from its cover. That implies a real diminution in the rights of all British citizens – a subtraction not an addition. In all the talk of curbing freedom of movement it is too often forgotten that leaving the European Union will also restrict the freedom of movement of British citizens, whatever the colour of new passports. For many people that restriction may be immaterial or only marginally irksome, but for others – such as students and researchers, a wide array of professions and countless businesses – it implies a major restriction in life's opportunities. Far from 'taking back control' it is a loss of my control over my life. That is much more important than the issue of which queue to join at an airport.

It is reassuring that this pre-Christmas PR stunt by the government has, it seems, fallen flat. Clearly, nostalgia ain't what it used to be.


## 21 January 2018

# Two Europhobes blink

*Suddenly some big name Brexiters get nervous.*

Everyone knows that 2018 is going to be a crucial year in deciding our future relationship with Europe, but with the nation – and the government – still divided it is still difficult to predict confidently how it will end. It is still impossible to see the shape of a 'framework deal'. The incompatibilities between the essentials of the European Union and our government's wish for a 'bespoke deal' still stack the odds in favour of a hard Brexit. A polished President Macron, more fluent in his English and his thinking than our own Prime Minister, offered no comfort on his visit last week. It is also hard to predict where the Labour's leadership's crab-like progress will take it. And only heavens knows in what ways the House of Lords will shred the Withdrawal Bill, even if it manages to give some succour to the Welsh and Scottish Governments.

Meanwhile, one portion of a tired British public just wants the gvernment to 'get on with it', even while others express an increasing nervousness about the outcome. That nervousness is at least catching, for the one thing you can safely say now is that this month two people blinked. First up, our saloon bar Saladin, Nigel Farage, closely followed the Bullingdon bugle, Boris Johnson. Mr Farage, worried that Remain forces seem increasingly to be commanding the argument, started musing on television about a second referendum to silence them forever. He also knows the party he led is imploding.

A few days later Mr Johnson – lest we forget, our Foreign Secretary – let it slip (admittedly according to *The Sun*) that he might prefer to stay in the EU than have a Norway-style soft Brexit in which we would 'take' the EU rules rather than help 'make' them. Mr Farage's statement was a recognition that those arguing for us to Leave the EU are now on the back foot in terms of the argument, even if not in terms of a hold on the levers of power.

If *The Sun's* account is accurate, Mr Johnson – his views only slightly less tousled than his hair – is either admitting that the illusion of untrammelled sovereignty is more important to him than the livelihoods of British citizens, or that some power is better than none. If that were the choice, it is interesting to ponder just how Mr

Johnson would engineer our return to the EU fold – another referendum perhaps. But if we need a new referendum to choose between a soft Brexit and the status quo, why would we not need one to choose between the status quo and a hard Brexit? As someone always capable of rising above principle, doubtless these concerns will not keep Mr Johnson awake at night.

Now these may be straws in the wind, but this month I also felt another indication that the wind may be beginning to blow from a different direction – an audience of more than a hundred and fifty turning out on a Friday night at Aberdare Community School to listen to a lecture by a distinguished academic, Anand Menon, Professor of European Politics at King's College, London. Aberdare is in the heart of Rhondda Cynon Taf that voted 53.7%-46.7% for Leave, a majority of 8,617. The Cynon Valley is a more open, expansive valley than those either side of it. Yet that softer feel is belied by just as many closed shops in the town centre, life expectancy that is fully ten years less than London's surbubia, and a third of the population taking anti-depressants.

Professor Menon and his colleagues run a research project – The UK in a changing Europe – designed to put objective information on this issue into the public domain. (See www.ukandeu.ac.uk) His presentation was, at one and the same time, passionate and dispassionate. He believes that a hard Brexit will involve a massive hit to our trade with the EU – a 3% annual reduction in the economy for as far ahead as one can see. He also questions whether the mooted end date of December 2020 for a transition period allows sufficient time to complete such complex trade talks, to get new customs arrangements up and running and to get the necessary legislation in place for areas such as agriculture and immigration. He argues, therefore, for an extension of the Article 50 period of negotiation on the basis that "doing Brexit right is more important than doing it quickly".

Professor Menon also had hard questions for those of us who would wish to remain in the EU. He could not see Remain Tories voting against any deal, for fear of a Corbyn government, nor the Labour leadership moving beyhond its current 'creative ambiguity' – an ambiguity that Carwyn Jones in Wales has had to go along with. And as for a second referendum, Professor Menon thought a narrow win for Remain might create mayhem in the country.

The problem with this line of argument is that it implies we are in a trap from which there is no way out, a political cul de sac. But political life is never like that. Stuff happens. A nation is not a rabbit caught in the headlights. On no possible analysis of the referendum debates and the result in 2016 can it be argued that the UK voted for a hard Brexit. And if that is where we are heading public opinion will change. In that situation, for those Tories torn between fear of Brexit-induced economic catastrophe and their nightmare of a Corbyn-induced one, another referendum may be an honourable way out.

Then, taking heed of Professor Menon's warning, the ground could be laid for a much bigger success. It would be a referendum distant from a general election, and, unlike in 2016, not complicated by proximity to elections to the devolved legislatures. In Wales, three of the parties could unite. It would be a referendum in which Jeremy Corbyn could no longer afford to shilly-shally. In such an election, no-one would be telling Leave voters they were wrong in 2016, they would be asking them to make up their minds on wholly new circumstances. The establishment or status quo that people would protest against, would not be the EU and Mr Juncker, but a government that had failed in its negotiations and failed the economy. My guess is the margin would not be narrow.

## 28 January 2018

## Is the carapace cracking?

*Public opinion refuses to shift, at least on the surface.*

When we look back in a year or more on the course of the Brexit drama will this last week be seen as the one when the tectonic plates began to move? The week when the glue that holds Theresa May's government together began to weaken, when Labour started to plan a more robust position and when the public mood showed unmistakable signs of fear?

Downing Street slap-downs for Philip Hammond and Boris Johnson within a few days of each other might be thought nothing new, especially in the case of the latter. A Bunter-like character will always be getting into and out of 'scrapes'. (Younger readers should Google Billy Bunter!) Mr Hammond's sin, in the eyes of the new Brexiter-in-chief, Jacob Rees-Mogg, was to express himself in an understated way that used to be regarded as very British, but is out of fashion in the current partisan climate. To want to move our economy only 'modestly apart' from our largest customer might in more normal times be regarded as common sense, but in days of passionate intensity apparently it just won't do.

The hard Brexit mobsters have not yet pulled the rug from under their own Prime Minister, but approaching forty-eight of them are taking up a white-knuckled grip on the rug's edge. Living tantalisingly within sight of their promised land, impatience will eventually push them to rash deeds, perhaps sooner than we think. For them, 2019 must seem like an eternity away. It seems this frustration is no longer confined to a wild-eyed fringe. Frustration at Theresa May's colourless leadership is now inducing a wider despair – not only at her brittle style, but at the lack of policy substance: no clear idea of where she wants to end up on Brexit, and no follow through on her long succession of vaguely empathic phrases about those suffering most and longest from the country's many ailments.

At the same time, Labour may be beginning to realise that, given its stubborn failure to establish a clear lead in the polls, the country is not guaranteed to drop into the party's lap in the event of election. Not only is its 'creative ambiguity' beginning to pall, it is increasingly out of step with its own supporters. An ICM survey published at the weekend made this as a plain as a pikestaff, which may be why Jeremy Corbyn, in his interview with Andrew Marr, inched towards commitment to staying in the EU's customs union, albeit still retaining his dogged ambiguity by referring to 'a form of customs union'. He is still resistant to another referendum but he is, as celebrities tell us these days, on a journey, the next stop on which may well be a Labour leadership awayday next month to review its position on Europe.

One must hope that at that event the shadow Secretary of State for Wales, Christina Rees MP, will hold true to her strong European convictions. She would also do well to polish up the the art of judo at which she excelled in her youth. (It will be interesting, too, to see whether Carwyn Jones gets an invitation.) She will be able to remind Mr Corbyn that he cannot forever ignore the fact that 77% of Labour voters think the public should have a chance to take a final decision when negotiations are complete, compared with 58% of the population as a whole and 59% in Wales. Even amongst Labour supporters who would vote Leave, 39% are now in favour of a new referendum.

To give Mr Corbyn the benefit of the doubt, the ICM poll does illustrate the current paradox: that while the top line Leave/Remain preference is stubbornly balanced (51-49 in favour of Remain), the unmistakable view of the public in general, and Labour voters in particular, is that Brexit will be bad for the economy. For all voters, 49% think the economic consequences will be negative, and only 36% think they will be positive. But no less than 66% of Labour voters say it will be negative and only 20% positive. 50% of Labour voters think it will also be bad for their personal finances and 57% think that there will be a negative impact on British life in general.

As for opinion in Wales, the results have to be heavily qualified as only 270 of the weighted base of 5075 were polled in Wales. Nevertheless, 48% in Wales thought the impact on the economy would be negative, against only 34% who thought it would be positive. Only 20% in Wales thought the impact on their personal finances would be positive, against 38% who think it will be negative. On the issue of Europe the starkest dividing line remains age, far more so than social class. If there were another referendum tomorrow 73% of eighteen- to twenty-four-year-olds would vote to Remain, compared with 38% of the sixty-five to seventy-fours and 31% of the those above seventy-five. The biggest increase in those who would vote Remain is amongst students, an increase of 16%. Only the sixty-five plus cohorts still register a majority for leaving the EU. As for class divisions, every social class is in favour of a referendum on the final deal, while only in the DE category does a majority think the impact on the economy wil be positive, and then only by 42-40.

When faced with this overwhlemingly negative view of the consequences of Brexit for the economy, the country and personal finances, is it then really credible that the Leave dam will hold, unchanged, for as long as it takes to negotiate an agreement? Underneath the carapace of a settled view of the binary choice between Remain and Leave, is a sinkhole of worry, not to say despair. At some point that carapace will crack. The only issue is whether it will give under the weight of governmental dysfunction and failure, or the pressure of opposition leadership yet to manifest itself fully, or just collapse from sheer fatigue.

## 22 February 2018

# Down the mine without a canary

There was a chorus of complaint over the last weekend at an apparent lack of clarity about the government's position on our future relationship with Europe. Strange, given that 10 Downing Street made its most unequivocal statement to date: "It is not our policy to be in *the* customs union. It is not our policy to be in *a* customs union." We should be absolutely clear what those two categorical sentences mean: this government is no longer governing in the national interest.

In those twenty-two words Her Majesty's Government has set aside both principle and a mountain of evidence to maintain itself in office and to mollify a small group of Conservative MPs who do not command a majority in their own party let alone in the House of Commons or the country. It is to caricature the results of the referendum in order to conform with the wishes of a bullying clique. It is saying, in effect, that its dominant objective is to hold its grievously split party together, regardless of its lack of any discernible alternative plan for the future of the country, regardless of the undeniably deleterious impact on the country's economy and finances, regardless of its toll on the livelihoods of people and whole regions, and regardless of the declared views of the elected governments of Scotland and Wales and that of our closest neighbour, Ireland.

It means that the Welsh Government's desire for "full and unfettered access" to the single market has been set aside, despite the fact that 61% of Welsh exports and more than 90% of our agricultural exports are to the EU. It ignores the 'just-in-time' requirements of British industries whose processes are intricately inter-woven with those of European partners. And it turns a deaf ear to the ticking clock that is counting us down to a destination still unknown and unfathomable. The best that any government representative has been able to offer is the prospect of an undefined 'customs arrangement', a concept that lacks all shape – other than that of a fag packet – and abjures coherence, simplicity and certainty in favour of uncertainty, fragmentation, complexity and cost.

One Conservative spokesman, in another triumph of hope over experience, has said that in such a situation "it is not beyond the wit of man" to find some technological solution to the policing of our borders. Perhaps, but so far it appears to be beyond the wit of this government. The examples of NHS data and universal benefit are not exactly encouraging. We are left with the more real prospect of Kent and the Isle of Anglesey being clogged with lorries, that is until our trade with Europe has, inevitably, subsided. The consequences for Northern Ireland are even more serious, and potentially tragic.

In a statement of the obvious, yet one to which our own government appears deaf, M. Barnier, the EU negotiator said on his London visit, "The only thing I can say, without a customs union and outside the single market, barriers to trade in goods and services are unavoidable." It is in this situation that Brexiters ask us to place our faith in their cloudy crystal ball, while at the same time criticising civil servants for at least making an attempt to quantify the risks, and in so doing honouring the Civil Service Code. This code requires them to "take decisions on the merits of the case" and to "provide information and advice on the basis of the evidence".

Let us be more precise. Conscientious officials, working to the government, can see no foreseeable Brexit scenario in which the economy, jobs and the public finances are better off. Even within a single market and customs union, their assessment is that our economy would shrink by two per cent, cutting jobs by 700,000 and giving the Chancellor £15 billion less in his kitty each year. Outside the single market and customs union – but with a hoped-for comprehensive free trade agreement – the economy would shrink by five per cent, reducing jobs by 1,750,000 and the public finances by £37 billion a year. In the event of a no deal scenario – that Mrs May once thought was better than a bad deal – the economy would shrink by eight per cent, cutting jobs by no less than 2,800,000 and the public purse by £58 billion a year.

Play around with these assumptions as you will, it is impossible to conjure a plus on any front. No reputable economic agency or think tank has managed to do so. You would think that these figures would at least counsel caution. And yet the Government feels the need to listen to Mr Rees-Mogg and his band of brothers who would have us brush them aside, preferring to send us into an uncharted mine without a Davy lamp or a canary.

In what conceivable way can this course of action be judged to be in the interests of the country as a whole, let alone in the interests of Wales, and especially its poorer parts? More urgently, on what conceivable grounds can this be judged to be an acceptable proposition for the Leader of the Opposition and his party? If this isn't a moment when 'clear red water' divides the Labour party at Westminster beyond any doubt from the government, then what will bring that day about?

It is the Prime Minister who said that she wanted to govern 'for the many and not the few', and who professed to want to unite a divided country. She is now committing to a course that will hollow out her own words, not to mention the lives of countless thousands. Mrs May, in the words of one of your predecessors, "No. No. No."

## 14 February 2018

# A gnarled and lifeless olive branch

Boris Johnson has made a speech. Apparently, it is an important one. Message to self: Resist the temptation to play the man not the ball, however many invitations he may issue daily. Take off your partisan ear-muffs and listen carefully to what he is saying. He is, after all, Her Britannic Majesty's Secretary of State for Foreign Affairs. Try to understand. Here goes.

We have been told that the Foreign Secretary's speech is the first of six to be given over the coming weeks by a select group of Cabinet Ministers that, strangely, does not include the Chancellor of the Exchequer, the keeper of the nation's finances. This setting out of the Government's position by instalments is either a bow to the fact that its position is still a work in progress, or a bow to the fashion for box sets. I leave you to judge.

Mr Johnson's expressed and honourable intent was to reach out to Remainers. He acknowledged that the vast majority of Remainers "are actuated by entirely noble sentiments, a real sense of solidarity with our European neighbours and a desire for the UK to succeed." His aim was to show that, contrary to the belief of most Remainers, "Brexit can gratify those sentiments – and more." He wanted to tackle what he sees as three mis-conceptions about Brexit. First, that leaving the EU is a "geo-strategic mistake" and weakens the security of the whole of Europe. Second, that by voting to leave the EU we have "sundered ourselves from the glories of European civilisation" and voted for "nationalism, small-mindedness and xenophobia". Third, that we have "voted to make ourselves less prosperous". Did he manage to pull the rug from under those three mis-conceptions? Let's take each in turn.

In dealing with the allegation of a geo-strategic mistake and European security, he was certainly convincing in setting out Britain's continuing commitment to the defence of Europe that, he said, was "unconditional and immoveable". The fact that we represent 13% of the EU's population but contribute 20% of defence spending is certainly telling. However, he made no mention at all of any other aspect of our geo-strategic positioning and influence. He was totally silent on the issue of whether the EU, representing nearly 7% of the world's population, or the UK with only 0.87% would have the greater influence in a world dominated by economic giants, whether states – like the USA, China or India – or multi-national companies like Google, Facebook, Apple and Amazon. If I was marking his exam paper, I would say he did not answer the question that he himself set.

The second question – whether we are about to sunder ourselves from the rest of European civilisation – is, admittedly a matter of judgement. One would have to accept the implied thrust of his argument, namely that cultures and civilisation often transcend the vagaries of politics and the rise and decline of states. Tourism will not end. We will still watch Scandi-noir television series and no doubt the rest of Europe will watch the odd Cymru-noir series in return. Brits will still struggle to learn other European languages, largely as a result of our own insular education policies. But Mr Johnson moved on to what might be called the "no taxation without representation" argument and quoted the 19th century philosopher John Stuart Mill in defence of the proposition that only national solidarity can legitimate the state and the burden of taxation. Even if there is something in that argument, the question is whether it is relevant to the issue at hand.

First, let's get some perspective and take a monetary measure. In 2017-18 total UK public expenditure will amount to £814 billion. Britain's net contribution to the EU budget will be £7.3 billion, or less than 0.9 per cent. This is hardly evidence of the existence of a European super-state. The EU is not a super-state. It is a coming together of sovereign states that have decided to pool some of their sovereignty for their own greater good.

The notion that the EU is some Leviathan on which we have had no influence and which threatens our democracy and sense of national identity does not bear much examination. Mr Johnson's statement that "it would be absurd if we were obliged to obey laws over which we have no say and no vote" is a statement of the obvious. However, it does not describe how the EU operates. Yes, there are some legitimate questions about how we might inject a greater democratic element into the operation of the EU, and some of the solutions posed in recent years have foreseen a larger role for national Parliaments. But Mr Johnson's argument denies the existing dominant role and influence of elected national governments.

In his view every decision becomes an "imposition". Obeying laws our own representatives have agreed, and which have facilitated continental trade, becomes "having to comply with some directive devised by Brussels" or being "lashed to the minute prescriptions of a regional trade bloc". His view of the economic issue is similarly political, and sometimes his arguments trip each other up. Only Brexit, he says, will allow us to move from a low wage, low productivity economy to a high wage, high productivity economy. Only Brexit will allow our entrepreneurs to innovate. Only Brexit will allow us to exploit changes in the world economy. Have British governments really carried no responsibility on all these matters over the years?

But then he argues that our sales to many countries outside the EU have risen sharply since 2010. Indeed they have. Would you believe, that has been achieved by our allegedly chained entrepreneurs even while remaining part of the EU. Germany has done even better. The truth is that selling to the EU and to the rest of the world is not a zero sum game. Getting the best for Britain should mean a both/and strategy, not either/or. Worst of all, Mr Johnson is explicit in saying we should not worry about coming out of the single market and customs union –

although he carefully avoids a recommendation – and, in a circumlocution characteristically devoid of numbers or precise meaning, says that "the economic benefits of membership are nothing like as conspicuous or irrefutable as is sometimes claimed". He is clearly not averse to a hard Brexit.

In reaching out to Remainers, I'm afraid that he has offered a gnarled and leafless olive branch. And, unsurprisingly, he has certainly not reached out to the 'left behind'. We shall see whether another five ministerial speeches can do any better.

## 17 February 2018

## Starmer's six tests

An evangelical centre in Cardiff was a strange place for a Labour Party 'Brexit Summit' yesterday. Across from the main hall is a baptism pool, presumably for those who have not already been baptised as true believers in the gospels according to Remain and Leave. There were not many takers – for baptism that is. This being Cardiff, a white-collar, solidly Remain city, most of the audience had gathered in the hope that Keir Starmer would bring them some comfort about his 'slowly, slowly, catchy monkey' task of reining in his own leaders scepticism.

Sadly, they were disappointed, a disappointment sharpened by the fact that his ration of caution came hard on the heels of a barn-storming speech by the Welsh Finance Minister, Mark Drakeford. Mr Drakeford, a former academic, has a reputation as the most cerebral member of the Welsh Cabinet and, I guess, more than a match for a script-bound Mrs May across a negotiating table. He is not known for tub-thumping, but this afternoon he was on fire. Mr Starmer, alas, was not and was roundly barracked by many in the audience for his insistence that "you cannot ignore the result of the referendum".

He is, of course, the deviser of the Labour Party's six tests against which it intends to measure any deal that the government presents to Parliament in the autumn of 2018. He set out these tests nearly a year ago in March 2017. In form they echo the five tests that Gordon Brown set out in 1997 for assessing whether the UK should join the Euro or not, although Brown claimed that these did not deal with the political issues involved. In the case of the tests for the Euro, Brown came to a definitive conclusion and we did not join. Will Starmer's tests for the Brexit deal elicit as clear-cut an answer? We must hope so, although there is wriggle room in some of them.

The decision on the Euro was different. Whether or not to join the Euro posed a binary question: you would either be in the Euro or not. You could not be half in or half out. Neither was there a choice between a hard Euro or soft Euro. Some on the right have argued that these six tests for a Brexit deal are ones that Theresa May can never pass. Maybe. Some of the tests will certainly involve fine judgements – what might satisfy Theresa May may not satisfy Anna Soubry and what may satisfy Jeremy Corbyn might not satisfy Chuka Umunna – but, a year later, the outcomes of other tests do seem pre-determined, and justifiably so. This is not the result of political prejudice so much as an inescapable response to facts already known. What are those tests?

### 1. Does it ensure a strong and collaborative future relationship with the EU?

This is a vague formulation that is not easily measurable. 'Strong and collaborative' involves value judgments. As long as the talks do not collapse before autumn 2018 – and this now seems unlikely – there will be some sort of framework deal to put before Parliament, although it will be hard-pressed to measure up to Theresa May's rhetoric about "a deep, special and comprehensive relationship". Even if no deal can possibly be as comprehensive as the one we have had for forty-five years, Mrs May is bound to try to sell whatever she ends up with as the basis for a sound future relationship. The absence of the kind of detail that the next twenty-one months of negotiations are meant to sort out, will allow her a lot of leeway in arguing the case. But it may also test Jeremy Corbyn's proclivity for turning a blind eye to awkward facts.

### 2. Does it deliver the "exact same benefits" as we currently have as members of the Single Market and Customs Union?

It is very difficult to see how any agreement can possibly pass this test, particularly since the UK has ruled out a Norway-style deal. The words 'exact same benefits' are precise and challenging. They cannot be fudged without a level of disingenuousness that would be screamingly obvious to all. Carwyn Jones, Wales' First Minister, has long argued for "full and unfettered access to the single market", and Keir Starmer has said he wants the benefits of both the single market and the customs union "hardwired into the final agreement". Yet it is surely impossible for the EU to deliver the 'exact same benefits' without undermining the union itself. We know already that M. Barnier is duty bound to deliver something less than the status quo. This means that the answer to this test is known now – it will fail – even if the extent of the shortfall between aspiration and outcome will depend on another two years of negotiation.

### 3. Does it ensure the fair management of migration in the interests of the economy and communities?

This is clearly the issue that exercised many of the core Leave communities, even in constituencies, such as those in the south Wales valleys, where immigration levels are in reality very low. Remainers generally and Labour in particular have been searching for an answer that responds to that level of concern while not compromising liberal and internationalist instincts. There are, surely, routes through this issue. One has been suggested by Hywel Ceri Jones, a former Director General in the European Commission, who is now a member of the Welsh Government's European Advisory Group. He argues that the EU's past positions on this issue have been much more helpful than a hostile press and the ranks of Europhobes have been prepared to admit. He points to Articles 48 and 49 of the original Treaty of Rome as well as to the agreements reached with David Cameron in his pre-referendum negotiations.

Article 48 of the Treaty of Rome stated that "freedom of movement for workers shall entail the right (a) to accept offers of employment actually made (b) to move freely within the territory of member states for this purpose." But Article 48 was qualified by the following Article 49 which stipulated that the EU could set up appropriate machinery to facilitate the achievement of "a balance between supply and demand in the employment market in such a way as to avoid serious threats to the standard of living and level of employment in the various regions and industries." These articles were echoed in the agreement hastily negotiated by David Cameron only four months before the 2016 referendum. This stated that free movement "may be subject to limitations on grounds of public policy, public security or public health." For good measure it added that free movement could be restricted by "measures proportionate to the legitimate aim pursued" and specifically included in such legitimate aims "encouraging recruitment, reducing unemployment, protecting vulnerable workers, and averting the risk of seriously undermining the sustainability of social security systems".

The deal with Cameron may have been taken off the table in light of the referendum result, but there is clearly no obstacle in principle to reviving it or a version of it. As Jones says, "Free movement is not and never has been uncontrollable by Member States. There is ample scope in the present negotiations with the EU to reach a formal understanding that could respect the views of all Member States."

### 4. Does it defend rights and protections and prevent a race to the bottom?

Given the nature of the EU Withdrawal Bill, the UK government will no doubt be arguing that that these

178

rights and protections have been defended by their wholesale translation into British law. That is to miss the crucial point. Ultimately, this test comes down to a question of trust in our own political system and UK Government intentions, subject to any continuing but time-limited jurisdiction by the European Court of Justice. Short of disaster in the negotiations, Mrs May will argue that the test has been met, while Labour will rightly ask, but for how long? Those like Roger Scruton who fret about sovereignty argue that treaties "lie on the legislative process like a dead hand." A more positive view is that the EU has given the rights and protection of workers an immensely valuable guarantee against the excessive partisanship of British politics, as well as long-term stability for both employers and employees.

## 5. Does it protect national security and our capacity to tackle cross-border crime?

Eventually it should be possible to see clearly whether or not this test has been met, despite the many dimensions of the issues involved, but, again, how clear will the situation be by October or November 2018, rather than at the end of 2020? Post Brexit will we still be stitched into Europol, or will we have a seat outside the door? Will we still be party to European Arrest Warrants? Above all, will we have found a solution in Ireland that guarantees continued peace, and a renewed impulse towards reconciliation. During her speech to the Munich Security Conference today May called for a special partnership on security, and the guidelines to EU negotiators call for "strong EU-UK cooperation in the fields of foreign, security and defence policy." However, there seems little likelihood that detail in all these spheres can be completed before the "meaningful vote" in autumn 2018, since there are also differing views among the EU 27. Significantly, in the published transition agreement the sections on security are not among those colour-coded in green.

## 6. *Does it deliver for all regions and nations of the UK?*

"Delivering for all the nations and regions" can mean different things to different people. Keir Starmer will need to be more specific. The only measurable concept in this wording is the word – 'all'. We should not lose sight of that small word. Taken at its face value, it means the test should not be satisfied by assessing some balance of advantage to be struck across the UK, but rather by a commitment to each and every nation and region. It is not beyond measurement. We know exactly what the cash benefits of EU membership are for the nations and regions of the UK under the structural funds and the CAP. We know which nations and regions are net beneficiaries. Each area knows what it stands to lose. Of the four countries of the UK, Wales has been the major beneficiary of structural funds, being awarded a fifth of all the funding to the UK. The per capita figures for 2014-2020 will be: England £13, Scotland £18, Northern Ireland £30 and Wales £83. The figure for England masks substantial regional variations, but the allocations have been based on precise measures of their respective economic circumstances. It is as certain as night follows day that a centrally driven regional policy shaped by the UK Treasury will seek to flatten these disparities, no matter that they are evidence-based. The UK's raw politics will trump evidence rather more often.

The multifarious impacts of any UK-EU deal within each nation and region will also vary depending on their particular industrial structures and specialisms as well as the agricultural characteristics of each place. The cherries, if there are any, are unlikely to be evenly distributed. But just as important as the substance of any deal with the EU will be the approach of the UK Government and the devolved administrations towards agricultural support, as well as the extent of the UK Government's commitment to robust regional policies: not mere gestures towards the mitigation of economic disadvantage but a resolute long term commitment to re-balancing the UK and reducing regional disparities. To do so the interaction of the two levels of government will have to be more constructive than the UK Government has allowed it to be to date.

Things do not look promising. Ministers have already refused to promise a one hundred per cent replacement of levels of funding received via the EU's structural funds, and Michael Gove has already touted plans for radical changes to agricultural support that, though they may stop short of the cold turkey that was inflicted on New Zealand farmers in the 1980s, will have unpredictable impacts given the widely differing characteristics of our agricultural areas. A place like Wales is particularly at risk on the agricultural front where small farms predominate and much of it is upland farming. The devolved administrations will reserve the right to shape agricultural policies of their own, but they will need the financial resources to do that.

Neither, despite its supposedly inclusive title, can one be confident that the scale of funds allotted to the new UK Shared Prosperity Fund will be of the necessary order, or that the approaches of the two levels of government will be effectively complementary. History is the best pointer. UK Governments have never been enthusiastic promoters of regional policies, apart from a twenty-year period after the Second World War. Active instruments of regional policy were largely abandoned by the end of the 1970s, and have never been revived. It has been a different story in Europe, where the aim of "strengthening economic and social cohesion" has been an indelible statutory objective of the EU since the Treaty of Maastricht in 1992. From 2014-20 the EU's cohesion policy will be the second largest budget item, claiming €352 billion of the total. There is no parallel guiding rubric nor comparable funding to be found anywhere in the UK's squidgy constitution or the Chancellor's plans.

Professor Kevin Morgan of Cardiff University, an expert on regional policy across Europe, has already expressed concerns about the UK Government's new industrial strategy, where the balance between sectoral approaches and place-based approaches has yet to be resolved. "Sectoral deals", he says, "tend to play to existing strengths and this constitutes a major dilemma for poorer regions and nations, which lack the critical mass, the political traction and the social network connections through which deals are aired and developed in bilateral exchanges with the UK Government." His view is that "place should be the overarching and integrating theme in the industrial strategy, not simply a theme among many others." In the light of the UK

Government's characteristic reluctance to contemplate dealing with the devolved administrations on equal terms, he is not optimistic.

This particular test will not only challenge the current government, it will also challenge Labour to step up to the plate with a new approach to decentralisation. Taking a leaf out of Gordon Brown's book – one of his tests for economic and monetary union – perhaps Keir Starmer should add a seventh test for any Brexit deal: Will it "promote higher growth, stability and a lasting increase in jobs."

## 22 February 2018

# Ireland – the perils of amnesia

There is a Welsh feeling for Ireland that runs deeper than feelings for any other part of the British archipelago, other than our own. Despite the closeness of our ties with England – certainly economically and socially closer than those with Ireland – history, language and the unbridgeable disparity in size between Wales and England inevitably induces ambivalent feelings. Welsh warmth towards Ireland is unqualified.

It's also catching. At the end of a business function in Cardiff last week, a businesswoman, English by birth but now well stitched into the Welsh community and distraught at the prospect of Brexit, asked me a very surprising question. "Tell me," she said, "can our National Assembly declare war?" "Why?" said I. "Well, if we can, we could declare war on Ireland – and lose.

Then we could join them." I daresay the constitutional lawyers will give this novel idea rather short shrift. But the jest does speak of a common spirit between the two small nations that accentuates our horror at a too common English amnesia about its own tortured relationship with the Emerald Isle.

A week ago our Foreign Secretary, Boris Johnson, in the first of a series of heralded ministerial speeches on Brexit, managed not to refer to Ireland or Northern Ireland even once – not a single syllable. This is not only a Brexiter trait. In his book *Unleashing Demons, The Inside Story of Brexit*, Craig Oliver, David Cameron's Director of Politics and Communications right through the referendum period, managed the same trick. Not a word in 408 pages. The words Ireland, Northern Ireland and Stormont appear nowhere in its index, neither will you find the name of a single Irish Taoiseach. If English amnesia about Irish history is the first unforgiveable sign of insensitivity, the second is its continuing marginalisation in the Brexit context, while the third is a wilful disregard for the likely economic impact of Brexit on our closest neighbour. Do not underestimate the sense of injury.

For if the British economy is impossibly inter-twined with the rest of Europe, that is doubly the case when you look at the linkages between Britain and Ireland. These multitudinous interconnections between the two economies have been examined by the Irish Institute of International and European Affairs, of which Daithi O'Ceallaigh is a former Director General. He is also a former Irish Ambassador to the UK and, previously, to the World Trade Organisation. He spoke at a Wales for Europe meeting in Cardiff last night.

He set out first the intricacies of the economic connections, fearing that Brexit might mean up to an eight per cent reduction in Ireland's GDP. Ireland is, understandably, by far the largest market for exports from Northern Ireland, and the island is increasingly one economic entity. But Ireland is also the UK's fifth largest market anywhere, and it is a market where the balance of trade is in the UK's favour. One third of Ireland's imports are from the UK. It imports ninety-three per cent of of its gas and eighty-nine per cent of its oil products from the UK. There is already a single all-Ireland energy market, with the electricity market in the north owned by the Irish state electricity board. Since 2001, the stability of its energy supplies has also been guaranteed by being physically linked to the UK's electricity and gas grids. This sense of economies inextricably connected applied, in his view, to banking, legal systems, aviation and most importantly, to food, where all the distribution centres for the dominant supermarkets are in the UK – such that a Marks and Spencer sandwich sold in Galway will have been buttered and filled on the opposite side of the Irish Sea.

He could also have mentioned (but did not) the newspaper business, since he was for some years the Chair of the Press Council of Ireland. One third of daily weekday newspaper sales in Ireland are Irish editions of UK newspapers, together with a fifth of Sunday newspaper sales, though it has to be said that their Irish editions take a very different editorial line from their London counterparts.

On the export side, too, forty-three per cent of all exports by indigenous Irish businesses go to the UK, including forty-two per cent of food and drink exports.

The UK also accounts for the largest share of Irish service exports.In totality, this means that Ireland's relationship with the UK is of a different order from that between the UK and the remainder of the EU's member states. Overall, a House of Lords committee recently concluded, "any potential negative impact of Brexit will probably be more significant for Ireland than for any other Member State, in particular, in the event of any economic downturn in the UK."[15]

All this, of course, could easily impact on Wales which is Ireland's main gateway to the UK and European markets. Every year more than 2.5 million passengers, to and from Ireland, as well as more than 530,000 lorries travel through Welsh ports, and seventy per cent of Irish cargo goes through Holyhead which is second only to Dover in the UK in the amount of roll-on and roll-off traffic. Failure to retain a frictionless border could turn Anglesey into a lorry park. Yet, surprisingly, there is no evidence of these consequences having beeen discusssed with the Welsh Government.

But it is in the field of peace and security that Daithi O'Ceallaigh had the greatest concerns. In the last week three Brexiter MPs – two Conservatives and one Labour – have poured scorn on the 1998 Good Friday agreement as if the problems of Northern Ireland were just an annoying impediment to the realisation of their personal prioritised dream. Owen Paterson says that the Good Friday Agreement has "outlived its usefulness". Daniel Hannan says derisively that the agreement is "often spoken about

---

[15] *Brexit: UK-Irish relations.* House of Lords European Union Committee. December 2016.

in quasi-religious terms". Kate Hoey, marginally more measured, has said that the power-sharing executive is not sustainable in the long term. It seemed to confirm O'Ceallaigh's view that "We didn't figure at all in the minds of the people who drove this referendum in England. We didn't matter. We didn't count."

Since the suspension of the Stormont power-sharing government is a serious matter, one would not wish to put the arrangement beyond debate, but this surely is a field in which politicians need to tread lightly and choose their words carefully. Northern Ireland is a place where a civil war on British soil cost 3,500 lives, and where another 47,500 people were injured. All that carnage in a space and amongst a population half the size of Wales. The hard won peace, achieved by the combined efforts of differing administrations in Britain and Ireland, was also endorsed by seventy-one per cent of the population of Nothern Ireland, although let us not forget that the DUP, paid sustainer of our present government, campaigned against it. In the parallel referendum in the Irish Republic ninety-four per cent endorsed the agreement. The GFA deals not only with the mechanics of power-sharing, but also with cooperation between the north and south of the island, and east-west between the Irish and British governments. It is an international agreement signed by two governments and underpinned by the EU, of which all parties were and, for the moment, still are members. It has also been supported by the EU's generously funded PEACE programme. This is not an issue or an agreement that merits cavalier treatment.

Last night, it was dispiriting to hear Daithi O'Ceallaigh having to remind his audience of all the perils Brexit could create for his own island, north and south. As someone who, as an Irish civil servant, was deeply involved in the tortuous negotiation of the GFA, he was conscious of both its centrality and its fragility. In that context he worried about "an introspection on the part of the English that is truly astonishing", about a sectarianism in the north that "is as deep as ever it was, and perhaps worse", and about the fact that the leaders of the DUP and Sinn Fein are now younger people who "have not come through twenty years of discussions and listening to the other side and who have both got themselves into the position where the only people they are concerned about are the people on their own side". For all these reasons he thought the implications of Brexit for his island were "horrendous".

He was blunt. "I am not for a moment saying that the provisional IRA are going to go back to war. They are not. But there are people within the republic – the dissidents – and those people are just waiting for an opportunity to start it all up again. And there are people on the loyalist side who are of the same mind. I have always taken the view that peace in Northern Ireland is going to take three generations, and three generations where the two governments together put their bloody feet to the fire to make sure both sides get on together."

I have heard some people – though not at the Cardiff meeting – dismiss the threat of a resumption of violence as blackmail, but that does not make it go away. If things go wrong again in Ireland, everyone will suffer. Does Britain never learn? The Irish dimension to Brexit is not just another issue in a checklist of matters to to be ticked off by negotiators. Of all the practical issues that Brexit throws up, this surely is the one where proposed solutions have to be the most watertight. This is not the place to test again the triumph of hope over experience, nor, for that matter, untested IT solutions. Neither is this some foreign clime. Our populations are as interwoven as our history. It is estimated that ten per cent of people in the UK, some six million people, have at least one Irish grandparent. More than 250,000 UK citizens live in Ireland. But even such figures, pressing as they are, do not speak to the moral dimension of this issue. We owe Ireland. Our contribution to Ireland's travails over the centuries is such that, at the very least, we should be obliged to resist any recurring amnesia not just from self-interest but as a matter of honour.

## 24 February 2018

## Self-praise is no recommendation

A round of applause, please, for David Anderson, Director General of the National Museum of Wales, for expressing so clearly his frustration with the hubristic obsession with the word 'Great' in Great Britain, to which fevered Brexiters and, rather too frequently, the British tourist industry are prone. He has come under fire for telling a conference on post-Brexit tourism, that he has no wish to stand under yet more banners proclaiming that 'Britain is Great'. I share his view. He has done us a favour. He has uncovered a truth and has received some brickbats for his pains from people who misconstrue this stance too easily.

To say that the title 'Great Britain', and its indiscriminate use in marketing and politics, is currently problematic, does not mean that the country's lauded achievements are a fiction, or that one is unpatriotic, or that one wants to talk Britain down, or that one has no faith in our capacity to shine in the world. It is, rather, an unwillingness to take marketing slogans and the heady perorations at political conferences at their face value. The latter are usually there not only to rally the faithful and to engender energy but also to elide harsher realities. If we are wont to laugh at Donald Trump claiming to 'make America great again', then we should be careful not to make the same mistake ourselves. Of all the moments in our history, this is not the one at which to encourage people to levitate above fact.

The problem arises from the fact that 'Great Britain' is a geographical description – dating back to Roman times – of the largest island in the British Isles, whereas it is now regularly used instead as a self-regarding value judgment. The equally ambiguous 'United' at least has the defence of legal fact. But this is what happens when you add adjectives to the names of countries. The truth is we have got ourselves into a mess with our own nomenclature, by attempting to reflect the union of English and Scottish crowns in 1603, the formal union of both countries in 1707, the union with Ireland in 1800, and the departure of the south of Ireland in 1922. As a result we are variously referred to as Britain, Great Britain, the British Isles, or the United Kingdom (of Great Britain and Northern Ireland) not to mention, uncomfortably often at home and abroad even in the 21st century, as England. 'United Kingdom' was not used until after the union with Ireland.

If you take your car across the English Channel you are required to display a GB sticker, even if you come from Northern Ireland, despite the fact that the term Great Britain does not include Northern Ireland. Of course, some regard tolerance of this kind of paradox – or muddle – as one of our country's glories. Up to a point, Lord Copper.

But this is more than a complaint about the historical clutter we have amassed across the centuries. You do not have to deny all that is good and praiseworthy in our past in order to argue that the existence of that adjective, Great, is currently distorting our worldview. You can sit in a Eurostar terminal in London and see our marketers riff on the word 'Great', or I should say 'GREAT', for it is always in capital letters. In current circumstances the very same display in the terminal at Brussels seems to thumb its nose even more at our European partners. As my mother would have said, "Self-praise is no recommendation."

In the current political and economic situation, it seems like an exercise in whistling in the dark: a deliberate masking of the weaknesses in our industrial performance, our declining productivity, and our ever negative balance of payments; a refusal to admit we are already poorer, a stubborn blindness to our true position in a world of economic giants, a determination to turn us, in reality, into Little Britain but to pretend otherwise. Of course there are things that we are good at. For instance, we can point to the creative and cultural industries, in which the United Kingdom is unarguably excellent, globally hugely influential and commercially successful. It is also a sector that has always been more solidly in favour of our engagement in Europe than almost any other group.

David Anderson is from that sector as well as from Northern Ireland, and more conscious than most of the dangers that complacency and fantasy solutions pose for peace on the island of Ireland. He is also no stranger to our high cultural productivity; indeed, he is a distinguished contributor to it and, in doing so, has been passionate in his commitment to take culture to those very same disadvantaged communities that registered their protest against their plight in the referendum. And he speaks for an institution, whose website address includes an abbreviation – .ac – that is used for universities and other academic organisations. It is the duty of academia, not just from time to time but consistently, to shake us out of the complacencies into which we are all inclined to slump.

One aspect of complacency is hubris. It is seen in spades in the ranks of the extreme Brexiters. They shun all arithmetic about the extent and intricacy of our economic connections with the rest of the EU, including our closest neighbour Ireland. They shun the arithmetic of regional imbalances within this country – by whatever name we wish to call it. And they shun the arithmetic of our comparative size in the world. To constantly play upon the world 'Great', is an excessive worship of a contested past and risks the most cruel deception of the people as regards our future.

## 7 March 2018

# A measure of contempt

Having applauded the Director General of the National Museum of Wales last week for calling out the excessive emphasis on the 'Great' in Great Britain in the Europe debate, this week's round of applause should go to the National Assembly of Wales and the Welsh Government for the introduction of its emergency 'Continuity Bill', and this for a number of reasons.

First, and sadly, one of the UK's youngest legislatures has had to take steps to mitigate the risks arising from the UK Government's cavalier attitude towards the devolved governments – risks that are posed not just to government but to business and wider society in Wales. The resulting Bill is also a sign of the cooperation between Labour and Plaid Cymru on Europe – that is not evident in Scotland between Labour and the SNP – as well as the energies of the Plaid spokesman on Europe, Steffan Lewis AM. It has prompted one Scottish journalist[16] to complain that Wales is making the running.

The Continuity Bill – more pedantically titled the Law Derived from the European Union (Wales) Bill – is designed to ensure that a huge legislative sink hole does not emerge under the government of Wales if the National Assembly is not able to give its consent to the EU Withdrawal Bill going through Westminster. It is clear from the Welsh Government's explanatory memorandum that this Bill has been presented reluctantly, as it would still prefer to be able to rely on Westminster's EU

---

[16] Iain Macwhirter, *Herald of Scotland*

Withdrawal Bill, but amended. The Welsh and Scottish Governments have felt compelled to produce their own Bills largely because of the UK Government's unwillingness or inability to deliver a timely response to their concerns.

Just consider the chain of events, or rather non-events, over the past year: the lack of any formal meeting of the Heads of Governments for more than a year; the lack of formal response by the UK Government to the white paper – *Securing Wales' Future* – prepared jointly by the Welsh Government and Plaid Cymru; the unfulfilled promise to bring forward suitable amendments to the EU Withdrawal Bill at Report stage – amendments still awaited.

The source of this problem lies in a consistent pattern of behaviour by successive UK Governments in relation to devolution. They have never had their hearts in the process. In his memoirs, Tony Blair seemed rather regretful about devolution, having pushed on with the legislation more out of loyalty to his deceased predecessor. The Cameron government did what it could to avoid having to enact in full the last-minute 'vow' of more powers that was made to the Scottish people in a state of panic when it looked as if the referendum on Scottish independence could be lost. As for Wales, Westminster, unable to conceive that Wales could exercise full legislative powers unaided, imposed a patronising system of legislative consent orders – LCOs – through which the National Assembly had to seek 'permission' to legislate, one piece at a time, from a glowering mother of Parliaments.

The 2011 referendum on legislative powers for Wales, won decisively by a margin of two to one, brought LCOs to an end, but despite this the long list of powers that Whitehall sought to reserve to itself was as comprehensive a scoping of central contempt for Welsh devolution as it is possible to imagine. Little wonder that the same mindsets are now struggling to find ways of minimising the role of the devolved governments in a post-Brexit Britain, insisting on handing out the sweeties of power at its own discretion and in its own time. The EU Withdrawal Bill actually amends the Government of Wales Act that gave Wales legislative powers, by preventing the National Assembly from modifying retained EU Law post-Brexit unless authorised to do so by an Order in Council approved by both Houses of Parliament – the return of LCOs with knobs on.

In the early years of devolution, the powers of the National Assembly were specifically conferred upon them. Anything not conferred remained at Westminster. The result in Wales was endless confusion about where precise powers lay. In Scotland, in contrast, clarity: all powers were transferred unless specifically reserved to Westminster. It is precisely that early confusing untidiness that an unamended EU Withdrawal Bill will recreate in Wales: powers conferred by devolution legislation, suddenly in partial or total abeyance. It is not a recipe for good government.

The UK Government is arguing that transferring all EU law to Westminster is a neat and tidy solution. The parcelling up of powers among the nations can be done later. This is superficial, disingenuous and bad politics. It is arguing, with all the condescension of people who enjoy the habit of power, that there is nothing to worry about. But it is a bit late in the day for the UK

Government to say to the governments of Scotland and Wales, trust us. It has form. The Welsh and Scottish answer must be, trust us instead.

In the Assembly debate on the introduction of the Continuity Bill these legislative slights were enough to prompt the remarkable sight of Neil Hamilton, the leader of the UKIP group, supporting the Welsh Government and lamenting the lack of understanding at Westminster. I suppose, no small achievement in itself.

The drafting of the Law Derived from the European (Wales) Bill and its very full explanatory memorandum has been no small feat. It demonstrates – along with various victories Wales has enjoyed in the Supreme Court in recent years – that in this legal field Wales can punch its weight. But it is sad that so much effort, expertise and legislative time has had to be expended in an attempt – and so far it is only an attempt – to extract from Westminster a modicum of common sense, fairness, respect and good manners.

# UNFINISHED BUSINESS

## 29 March 2018

A year to today, if the UK Government has its way, my country will leave the European Union after forty-six years and three months of membership. A valued part of the spectrum of my formal citizenship will be extinguished. Nearly half a century of working and growing together is to be cast aside, the stitching unpicked, the knitting unravelled so that we can stitch or knit or cobble something new for which we have no pattern or even idea in our heads, save a half-remembered mothballed garment a great-grandparent once wore.

If the British Empire was acquired in 'a fit of absence of mind', the next contested stage of the British journey was conceived in a nostalgic daydream. Not that one would want to belittle the past unnecessarily. It is, after all, a fascinating place. There are things to be proud of, things to cause an eyebrow to be raised, other things to be ashamed of. The past shapes us and our neighbours in ways that we can argue about, and in the process it can help shape our view of our present and future. It deserves the utmost respect, but that does not mean that one should worship it or want to live in it. History is but one context for our future, not its arbiter.

History is, of course, flexible. It can be pushed and pulled, tugged and stretched to construct narratives that, whatever their truth, serve some handy purpose in the present: to justify a specific stance or provide a psychological prop. There is little doubt that the historic dominance of the British Empire at one stage in our history, still colours the approach of many on the right, fuelling the aspiration to a global role as a revival of past glories. Hence the endless tropes about 'making Britain Great again'. It is not confined to those on the right. Its appeal means it even appears on the cover of Nick Clegg's book *How to stop Brexit (and make Britain great again)*.

Paradoxically, though the spirit of Empire still inhabits the subconscious of an older age group, particularly in England, the debate about Empire has scarcely impinged on wider public consciousness, active though it is amongst historians. There has been no national angst about the conduct of empire or the felt experience of its varied inhabitants. For nearly three-quarters of a century, incredibly, the angst has been focused instead on the parlous mental state of the erstwhile imperial power – a post-colonial melancholia, according to one author – a bruised self-absorption masked only by the cadences of our stiff upper-lip diplomats. In this regard we thought ourselves too busy and too proud to face up to our own history, as Germany had to do, in much more severe circumstances, after 1945. We have been more like the post-war French, in prickly denial. All this has shaped or rather expresses a predominantly English attitude towards

Europe. In the late Hugo Young's words – "The sense of the [European] Community as a place of British failure".

But England knows how to talk itself up – Shakespeare, Macaulay, Churchill. Modern philosophers too – supposedly more rigorous than conference speech-writers – can take a roseate view of our past. One such is Roger Scruton, a philosopher of conservative bent who, not content with a full blown elegy for England at the turn of the millennium, pursued his theme yet again last year in *Where We Are*, an assessment of 'the state of Britain now' – an attempt to assert the primacy of the nation state against the European project. It is a more sophisticated statement of the Brexit case than you will hear from campaigners, a beguiling book of flowing prose in which, as he himself admits, he "leans towards the more forgiving view of our national history, or at least the English part of it". He makes occasional allowances for Scottish nuances – less so for Welsh – but exults in the British habit of muddling through, our tolerance of paradox, our resolute amateurism, our preference for reasonable disarray above rational order, and above all our 'neighbourliness' as extolled in such works as *Under Milk Wood* and *Wind in the Willows,* not to mention *The Archers*. There is everything here save John Major's 'ladies cycling to communion'.

As is often the case with returning exiles – Scruton has spent much time in the Czech Republic and America – all change is regretted and, in this case, always characterised by tendentious description, whether it is 'the *gratuitous abolition* of our ancient weights and measures', or 'the *massive interference* of EU legislation in employment law and practice under the rubric 'health and safety'. At one and the same time the EU is criticised for being coercive – "the *stultifying restrictions* of the EU machine" and "its *hostility* to the national sentiments of ordinary people" – and permissive – "giving a kind of regulative *shelter to separatist parties* in Catalonia, Scotland and Flanders". By now some Catalans might take a different view of this last claim. [My italics]

And yet, few would question the importance that he ascribes to belonging. Belonging, he says, is the basic fact – its essentials: territory, sovereignty and "the day-to-day habits of neighbourliness". I doubt that many of us, whether we voted to Remain or Leave the EU, would quarrel with two out of the three. Personally, I am quite capable of getting misty eyed when driving over the crest at Dinas Mawddwy and seeing Cader Idris in all its glory before me. Contrary to popular belief, such emotions are widely felt far beyond the terraces of sports stadiums. The warmth of neighbourliness I have found ubiquitous and unmistakeable, in the north-east of England as much as here in Wales. So I feel no need for lessons in patriotism. Neither have I any wish to deny Mr Scruton his deep love of England, nor his desire for an English Parliament, even if, post devolution, it seems an exercise in me-tooism.

Sovereignty is another matter, and less hard-edged than Mr Scruton allows. His basic proposition, shared by many of the ideological Brexiters, is that the EU is "an aberration, a falling away from the great achievement of European civilisation in creating the sovereign nation state." Given the rivers of blood that have drenched European soil for some centuries past, and given the way that European wars have several times brought Britain to the point of national bankruptcy – at one time the result of having to pay other countries to prosecute war against Napoleon – some might think twice about an unqualified worship of the nation state. But there is another problem with Scruton's upmarket justification of the "take back control" slogan: his very English conflation of the state with nationality, "defined by borders, land and sovereignty." This is very much *de haut en bas* and he graciously admits that such nationality "does not extinguish local loyalties or the residue of older and more rooted ties". Whew!

But this toleration of difference, it seems, only extends in one direction, downwards. Because, he says, the EU cannot assume "the first person plural of nationhood... every move beyond the nation state, towards some transnational centre of government is a move away from democracy", although he does not rule out "transnational cooperation". One can argue about the theoretical and practical dimensions of democratic process within EU – the fact of elections, but the weakness of a European *demos* – but the reality is that transnational government in the EU is highly qualified.

In his book *Postwar* the late Tony Judt, a social democrat historian who was often trenchantly critical of the EU, put his finger on a paradox, a concept of which Roger Scruton is usually fond:

> "...for all its faults as a system of indirect government, the Union has certain interesting and original attributes. Decisions and laws may be passed at a transgovernmental level, but they are implemented by and through national authorities. Everything

> has to be undertaken by agreement, since there are no instruments of coercion: no EU tax collectors, no EU policemen. The EU thus represents an unusual compromise: international governance undertaken by national governments."

Judt does not imply that this represents a perfect state, but in view of the benefits associated with the European Economic Community and later the European Union, notably peace and prosperity, one might have thought this 'unusual compromise' – one might even say, a rather Anglican compromise – would have been up Roger Scruton's street, passing the test of 'reasonableness' on which he puts such store and avoiding a 'continental' application of reason, that Scruton regards as its 'single most important enemy'.

The truth is that a complacent sentimentality towards our imperial history, has distorted our view of the world, as well as of our own state. Pride in one's own country is a laudable sentiment, but excessive pride, tipping over into exceptionalism, risks dropping one's guard against delusions and self-deception. Jingoism requires blind spots. But this is to take a charitable view of some of the leading proponents of the Brexit cause. Too often their enthusiasm for Brexit is not so much worship of the Union Jack as cover for a hankering after a different kind of state, the raising of neo-liberalism's Jolly Roger. The treasure they seek to amass is not for distribution. The left behind can be, well, left behind.

This is also to pretend that the world is not as it is. Just look around. We have a narcissist in the White House who caricatures and demeans a nation that, at the best of times, has ever been robust in pursuit of its own interests and ever conscious of its power in doing so. For Trump a trade war is merely a virility test that he will need to be seen to win. Worryingly, he substitutes dangerous instinct for cool calculation, as we are seeing in his volatile dealings with North Korea. We have a more cunning narcissist in the Kremlin, who has a keen nose for vulnerability, is willing to feed Russia's traditional paranoia, to quash dissent at home and to wield an amoral power ruthlessly whether in Syria, the eastern Ukraine or on the streets of an English cathedral town. In China its president has just awarded himself life tenure, and is building a military as well as economic and financial capacity that is set to dominate the Western Pacific, and conceivably even threaten Australia. The reach of China's arm is long, whether into the bedrooms of its people or worldwide. For a measure of our negotiating power with China, just look at the grotesque deal on the Hinckley Point nuclear power station. In India we have a Prime Minister who has come from the ugly side of the sub-continent's politics, wishes to grow his country's economic power and, tellingly, is keener now to foster relations with the EU via Germany and France rather than with the UK. The UK's post-Brexit devaluation of the pound has meant that India's gross domestic product now exceeds that of the UK, two years earlier than forecast, while India's growth rate is six or seven times greater than that of the UK. It is in such a world that our government is intent on leaving the second largest economy in the world, six and a half times larger than our own, for the doubtful pleasure of paddling our own patched canoe alone into a boiling ocean.

This is to assess the power only of the giant states outside Europe that will largely shape our world. For in this globalised world it is with these states that we will have to negotiate our way through a period of disruptive change that is historically unprecedented: whether dealing with the unwelcome consequences of man's actions on climate change and borderless pollution of the air and the seas, or with the unpredictable consequences for people everywhere arising from man's creativity in genomics, artificial intelligence, automation and advanced robotics, or with the worldwide reach and excessive concentration of corporate power, evident in the hubristic quartet of Facebook, Amazon, Apple and Google. It is true that Britain has great scientific knowledge and diplomatic skills and has a contribution to make, but why would we trade only nominal control for effective power and influence? Why on earth would we scorn the augmented impact of our knowledge and experience that can be achieved by exercising it through both membership and perhaps quiet leadership of a whole continent? A European approach is not an inferior approach to a global one, it is the widest and fastest highway towards it.

Instead, abandoning the known and measurable benefits of our membership of Europe's unprecedented economic, social and cultural alliance, our rulers would have us embark on the greatest programme of useless displacement activity ever concocted by a British government, at a cost of not less than £3billion in cash and the creation of at least ten thousand unproductive bureaucratic jobs – needed to duplicate government departments and a host of regulatory agencies and to man hitherto frictionless borders. Even if Brexit were, in any sense at all, a 'nice to have', it would be a luxury we can ill afford, a massive and unending distraction from the legions of issues that await our attention.

If Brexit goes ahead in March 2019 we will embark on a difficult journey, first, of unavoidable decline and then, with luck, some recovery – a journey that will occupy two decades at the very least. Now a decade is a short time in which to bring about fundamental change. Recall that more than a decade after the last banking crash, Chancellors are still offering only the tiniest mitigation of austerity and this at the very moment our Prime Minister is finally confessing that "our access to each other's markets will be less than it is now." And while we are grappling with this prolonged and self-inflicted impoverishment over the next twenty years, the number of people of state pension age will rise by thirty-one per cent to sixteen million, while the numbers over eighty will double from three million to six million. These huge and inescapable demographic pressures pose a daunting enough challenge in themselves, not least for a health service that will continue to wait for the illusory £350m a week Brexit dividend. These pressures will make it all the more difficult – especially for a government committed to continued austerity – to bring forward policies that stand any realistic chance of narrowing the inequalities between and within our nations and regions, of raising our laggardly productivity, and of investing in the teachers and schools on which our future depends. At the same time we will continue to struggle to house our growing population, even in accommodation that has long not matched the space standards of previous generations, and yet remains unaffordable to most – thus lamentably failing in the most fundamental way the very generations that voted overwhelmingly to stay in the EU.

Despite this weight of evidence – not from experts but from the lived realities that we can all experience in our devalued pound, higher prices, our bulging A&E departments, our closing care homes and libraries, our pot-holed roads and the growing army of the homeless – despite all this, a flawed referendum has induced in our MPs and in many organisations striking displays of cognitive dissonance, that awful discomfort that comes from acting contrary to one's beliefs. Two obvious cases are the CBI and the Labour Party, though it is also far from uncommon on Conservative benches.

The CBI's most recent publication – *The Future UK-EU Relationship* – documents in enormous detail the problems that arise with any of the possible alternatives to our existing full membership of the EU: the Canada model, the Norway model, or a hybrid. It recognises the difficulty of negotiating a free trade agreement on services that it predicts will be "an unprecedented and uphill battle". It concedes that "the EU's economic heft means the balance of power when it comes to adopting rules sits with the EU". It admits that a Canada style deal "would inevitably lead to non-tariff barriers resulting in extra costs and delays for business". It states baldly that "no country has 'total sovereignty', except perhaps North Korea". It knows that "there is a trade off between weight and independence when it comes to rule making" and that "to sell to the EU businesses will have to abide by the EU's rules even if there is no deal". It cites the other problems of replacing the EU's cohesion funds in our more disadvantaged regions, and avoiding physical customs infrastructure at the Irish Border. And as for Britain negotiating trade deals with new markets, it says "there is simply not enough existing evidence to warrant endangering the existing frictionless trade of £145 billion in goods to the EU". All it lacks is the obvious conclusion. It is as if a packed express train of argument has stopped just short of the station.

The consequences of cognitive dissonance in the field of business may be less serious than in the field of party politics. Given the narrowness of the Government's majority, nowhere is this more important than within the Labour Party. Despite the fact that a large number of Conservative MPs voted Remain and would still prefer that outcome, it is unlikely that their convictions on Europe are going to be strong enough to smother either their loyalty to party or their fear of a Labour government. It is impossible to predict the scale of any Tory rebellion on a 'meaningful vote'. One can but hope it will be large enough. The apparent eclipse of the Liberal Democrats and the resumption of a two-party electoral battle – at least in England – means that the attitude of the Labour Party is going to be decisive. A large body of opinion has been praying that Labour stop tip-toeing around the issue and come out firmly in favour of staying in the EU, or at least in favour of a new referendum. Worryingly, in this early Spring of 2018, not only are the omens not promising but, last weekend, appeared to have been dashed altogether. The task ahead is to change that.

* * * *

Throughout 2017 Remain sympathisers in the Labour Party counselled patience, arguing that, given the state of public opinion, its best course was to adopt a stance of 'constructive ambiguity', that with luck might shadow changes in public opinion though never getting too far ahead of it. Last summer the party began to talk more positively about access to the single market and customs union, despite feeling it necessary to play around with the definite and indefinite article. Nothing was 'off the table'. It was only at the end of February this year that its leader committed to a policy of remaining in a customs union with the EU. Despite pleas from many parts of the party – the Welsh Government, the Mayor of London, the general secretary of the TUC, most trade unions and the party's Europe spokesman, Keir Starmer – Corbyn and Macdonnell are still resisting the notion of retaining *membership* of the single market. Nevertheless, until now we have been asked to believe that this was less important than the direction of travel.

On the weekend of 23-25 March 2018 this seemed to change. First Owen Smith, the party's spokesman on Northern Ireland, was sacked from the Shadow Cabinet for penning an article for *The Guardian* in which he dared to suggest that "we have a right to keep asking if Brexit remains the right choice for this country, and to ask too that the country has a vote on whether to accept the terms and the true costs of that choice once they are clear." On Sunday 25 March, Keir Starmer seemed to put all ambiguity aside in an interview with *The Observer*: "Article 50 was triggered a year ago. It expires in fifty-two weeks and a few days, and I don't think there is any realistic prospect of it being revoked. Therefore, we will be leaving the EU in March

2019." The only remaining ambiguity surrounded his dismissal of a 'Norway' option for the UK, despite also wanting to retain the benefits of the single market.

Although, overall, Labour is more sympathetic to Europe than the government party, pinning down its stance has been like putting a finger on mercury. This, surely, does not aid communication with the public or assist the national debate. Neither is it in its own interest. Surely, Keir Starmer's fear that the Labour party could divide and break up on this issue would only be valid if the party veered more towards more hardline support for Brexit? After all, there is a world of difference between the deep rift in the Conservative party and the differences of view in the Labour Party. In the former there is a crazed but formidable phalanx of extreme Brexiters for whom the severing of our links with Europe has been their life's work. The same cannot be said of the current Labour Party particularly, and ironically, after the explosion of membership during recent years. The primary rift is at the very top: Corbyn and Macdonnell on one side and Keir Starmer on the other, both sides drag anchors on the vessel of each others' true convictions.

Labour now has a membership, of which eighty per cent are in favour of staying in the EU. The proportion of its voters who share this view has risen from sixty-six per cent to seventy-three per cent in recent months. The overwhelming majority of younger members that are its future desperately want to remain citizens of Europe. Party insiders tell me that it is a gross misconception to think that Momentum members are like Militant of old, and that, despite their enthusiasm for Corbyn's leadership, they too would wish to stay in the EU. The complication, and the charitable explanation for such constructive ambiguity as still exists, is that seventy per cent of its Parliamentary seats are thought to be in areas where a majority probably voted to leave. This is the circle that Labour has to square. But it is at least arguable that if it jumps the wrong way, far from uniting the party, any rift could actually be deepened.

Why would a Labour Party, with its progressive social goals and its tradition of internationalism, want to take a fatalistic approach to the 2016 referendum result? There is absolutely nothing in that for the very people that Labour says it stands for. Every single thing a Labour government – whether in London or Cardiff or Edinburgh – might wish to do would be more easily achieved, and more effective in its application, if we were within the EU rather than outside it. If it wants to fix regional inequalities within the UK it needs the EU's cohesion funds. If it wants to address poverty in all its manifestations it needs every inch of financial headroom it can muster. If it wants to tame globalisation and to tackle the power of multinationals on tax or standards, it needs the clout of the EU (as we have seen with Apple and Google). If it wants to change the economic orthodoxies that have put such a heavy brake on growth and employment, especially in the UK and the countries of southern Europe, it needs change in the underlying policies not only of the UK but of the EU too.

And electoral risks? If the party were to go into the next general election not just with a lack of clarity, but also with a continuing commitment to abide by the 2016 result, the basis of which will almost certainly have come to look ridiculously outdated, would it really help its cause? If it were to be elected and have to implement Brexit, might it not also have set itself up for a truly torrid first term that could end up as its only term of office. Traditionally, Labour governments have struggled for credibility and trust on the economic front. In the early years of government they can face hostile market pressures that have a capacity to derail the best policy intentions. If Labour wants to implement a radical manifesto, then it needs the means to do so. It needs the most favourable economic climate it can engineer. That must surely mean rejecting Brexit.

So why, in such circumstances does the Labour leader, Jeremy Corbyn, continually perpetuate myths about Europe that seem to be a mirror image of the myths that have been peddled for decades by the Euro-hostile right? 'Blame Europe' is the trope, whether used by the right or the far left, that has got us into the mess we are in. It is surely high time it was discarded, since it is neither accurate nor constructive nor even cleverly ambiguous. Ambiguity, whether real or mythical, does not require or justify untruth. It is not a matter of the occasional slippery phrase. Take Corbyn's speech to the Scottish Labour conference at Dundee on 9th March 2018, the substance of which has been used in several of his speeches. I quote:

> "We cannot be held back inside or outside the EU from taking the steps we need to develop and invest in cutting edge industries and local business [and to] stop the tide of privatisation and outsourcing, or from preventing employers being able to import cheap agency labour to undercut existing pay and conditions in the name of free market orthodoxy.

"That's why we would want to negotiate protections or exemptions where necessary from current rules and directives that push privatisation and public service competition or restrict our ability to intervene to support domestic and local industry and business or undermine attempts to protect rights at work.

"It's striking that Theresa May's only clear priority when she laid out her new Brexit negotiating position last week seemed to be to tie the UK permanently to EU rules, which are used to drive privatisation and block support for British industry."

There are more than a few problems with this passage: it is either imprecise or just plain untrue, particularly in the implied EU restrictions on nationalisation and state aid. One academic assessment of the 2017 Labour manifesto by two lawyers, Andy Tarrant and Andrea Bondi, concluded that EU state aid laws "do not prevent a future Labour Government from introducing necessary radical reform of the British economy". Professor Anand Menon, who leads a fact-checking project on Brexit at King's College, London, has come to exactly the same conclusion.

Tarrant and Bondi examined the last Labour manifesto in detail: "Our assessment is that of the twenty-six specific economic measures...most (seventeen) do not even potentially fall within the scope of the State Aid rules. Of those that could, seven are likely to fall within block exemptions, for example, infrastructure spending is not an aid unless it directly competes with already privately funded infrastructure. This likely leaves only two measures which might have to be notified: the state investment bank/regional bank proposition and the state funded regional energy suppliers." These concerns of Jeremy Corbyn surely have even less validity when it is remembered that UK expenditure on state aid is vastly less than that of Germany or France, and that, in the Landesbanken and Sparkassen, Germany has long had a profusion of state banks.

Corbyn and Macdonnell's stubborn adherence to this myth of the EU as an obstacle to Labour's plans may be a legacy of their past, but today it is as inexplicable as Boris Johnson's refusal to disown the '£350m a week for the NHS' slogan on the Brexit battle bus. They need to climb to higher ground. It's not the case that Labour will not be able to do what it wants to do *if* it remains in the EU, but rather that it will not be able to do what it wants to do *unless* it remains in the EU. Even so, to be fair, every party will keep one eye on its electoral prospects, but if constructive ambiguity, based on a tone that has rarely been better than grudging towards the EU, were delivering a twenty-point lead for Labour in the opinion polls one might have to bow to the tactical genius of its leaders. But the fact is that not only did the party not win the last general election, but it is currently merely running neck and neck with one of the most disastrous governments since Lord North lost the American colonies. The British Election Study of the 2017 general election looked at the electoral impact of any possible shift in Labour's stance on Europe, and was exhaustingly inconclusive. Labour will have to take risks. No options are risk free, but neither do the risks look big. What we do know is that the current approach is akin to defending a 0-0 scoreline against a team on crutches.

* * * *

So, should we 'respect' the result of the referendum? Of course. But the greatest respect one can show to the result of the referendum is to understand what lies behind it, and the pain that propelled many communities towards their decision. Put aside for a moment the serious complaints about the mendacity of campaigns, the heavy suspicion of interference by 'dark money' and possible breaches of electoral law, and one is still left with the stark facts of stubborn and worsening individual and communal inequalities in our country. In Wales, the place I know best, it is not only the ten years since the last financial crash that counts, but the thirty years and more since the wiping out of coal and the shake-out in steel, industries on which so many communities were based – years in which neither UK governments that cared little nor, later, Welsh Governments that cared a lot have been able to engineer renewal and restoration. Even the extra resources from Europe, while aiding our public sphere in so many ways, have not touched individuals sufficiently in their own homes and lives – not at Brussels' direction but as a result of our own policies. To 'respect' the referendum, therefore, is not to be bound by it, regardless of changing circumstance. Questioning Brexit, even stopping Brexit, is not to disrespect those communities in Wales and elsewhere who voted to leave the EU, it is to respect the suffering that they have endured for far too long and to fear its prolonging. What should that respect entail?

In years to come, when people look back on this period between March and October 2018, they will recognise it as the last moment when the country and its elected representatives could still choose between a future buoyed up by continued membership of one of the greatest confederations in the history of the world – that is yet a work in progress – or a future where we will fidget on the fringes of everywhere – the perennial nuisance, sometimes indulged, more often not. If we take the latter path we will, no doubt, try to make the best of it, but we will not make the best of ourselves or of our country. We will have shrunk the garden in which our children and grandchildren will toil and play – and against their express wishes. We will have resurrected unnecessary borders on our shores and in our minds. We will have raised a tariff against neighbourliness. It is to prevent this fate that we must all bend our efforts over the coming months, not to retreat from the rest of the world but to make ourselves effective in it, not to resist democracy but to reassert it – through a new referendum. We need, at this time above all, to be the most active citizens. In all its tortuous dimensions and its pressing obligations, this is our unfinished business.

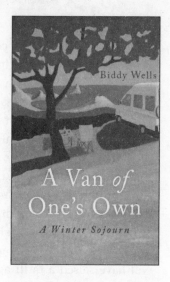
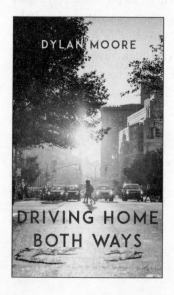
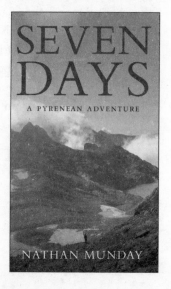